Corporate Acquisitions and Mergers in the Czech Republic

Corporate Acquisitions and Mergers in the Czech Republic

Second Edition

Lukáš Ševčík
Petr Měšt'ánek

Kinstellar, S.R.O.

&

Bohdana Pražská

KempHoogstad

This book was originally published as a chapter in Corporate Acquisitions and Mergers.

General Editor: Peter Begg

Wolters Kluwer

Published by:
Kluwer Law International B.V.
PO Box 316
2400 AH Alphen aan den Rijn
The Netherlands
E-mail: international-sales@wolterskluwer.com
Website: lrus.wolterskluwer.com

Sold and distributed in North, Central and South America by:
Wolters Kluwer Legal & Regulatory U.S.
7201 McKinney Circle
Frederick, MD 21704
United States of America
Email: customer.service@wolterskluwer.com

Sold and distributed in all other countries by:
Air Business Subscriptions
Rockwood House
Haywards Heath
West Sussex
RH16 3DH
United Kingdom
Email: international-customerservice@wolterskluwer.com

Printed on acid-free paper

ISBN 978-94-035-1780-3

e-Book: ISBN 978-94-035-1800-8
web-PDF: ISBN 978-94-035-1844-2

This title is available on www.kluwerlawonline.com

Printed in the United Kingdom.

KINSTELLAR, S.R.O.

Kinstellar is a leading independent law firm in Emerging Europe, Turkey and Central Asia, with offices in Almaty and Nur-Sultan (Kazakhstan), Belgrade (Serbia), Bratislava (Slovakia), Bucharest (Romania), Budapest (Hungary), Istanbul (Turkey), Kyiv (Ukraine), Prague (the Czech Republic), Sofia (Bulgaria) and Tashkent (Uzbekistan).

Operating as a single fully integrated firm, Kinstellar delivers consistently high-quality services across all jurisdictions in an integrated and seamless style. We are particularly well suited to servicing complex transactions and advisory requirements spanning several jurisdictions.

Our clients include leading international and regional corporations, banks and other financial institutions, state bodies, multilateral institutions, and international law firms with clients that require top-quality legal counsel in our jurisdictions. We handle the most important and complex assignments for clients across diverse industries and business sectors.

Kinstellar covers all aspects of domestic and international law, including Banking, Finance and Capital Markets, Competition and State Aid, Compliance, Risk and Sensitive Investigations, Dispute Resolution, Employment and Labour Law, Energy, Infrastructure and Projects, Intellectual Property, Life Sciences and Healthcare, M&A and Corporate, NPL's and Distressed Assets, Private Equity, Real Estate, Restructuring and Insolvency, Tax, Telecoms, Media and Technology.

Authors

This country chapter on Corporate M&A in the Czech Republic has been written by the following team of lawyers of Kinstellar Prague: Martina Březinová (Counsel) – *Regulatory Framework, Public Takeovers, Mandatory Bids*, Tomáš Čihula (Partner) – *Competition Law*, Petr Holub (Managing Associate) – *Labour Law*, Jan Juroška (Partner) – *Transformations*, Michal Kníž (Senior Associate) – *Anti-bribery and Anti-corruption Laws*, Petr Měšt'ánek (Head of Know-how) – *Regulatory Framework, Business Vehicles, Insolvency, Specific Issues of Company/Securities Law, Future Developments*, Adam Němec (Senior Associate) – *Intellectual Property Rights*, and Karla Rundtová (Of Counsel) – *Due Diligence*.

The country chapter has been reviewed and coordinated by Lukáš Ševčík, Managing Partner of the Prague office, and Petr Měšt'ánek, the Head of Know-how.

The tax and accounting sections have been written and edited by Filip Dostál (partner) and reviewed by Bohdana Pražská (partner) of KempHoogstad.

Kinstellar, s.r.o., advokátní kancelář

Palác Myslbek

Na Příkopě 19

CZ-117 19 Prague 1

Tel.: (420) 221 622 111

Fax: (420) 221 622 199

Web: www.kinstellar.com

Disclaimer

This document does not purport to contain a comprehensive summary of all the legal risks and issues in the legal areas it covers. It is to be used for information only and cannot be relied upon as legal advice, no legal or business decision should be based solely on this document.

Contents

LOCAL ECONOMIC, POLITICAL AND CULTURAL ASPECTS

General Comments on the Country Profile

[01] The Czech Republic is a country in Central Europe and comprises three historical territories: Bohemia, Moravia and Silesia. The Czech Republic occupies a key position at the crossroads of Western and Eastern Europe. Its neighbours are Germany to the west, Austria to the south, Slovakia to the east and Poland to the north. The total population of the Czech Republic is about 10 500 000 people. The capital city of the Czech Republic is Prague, with population of about 1 240 000 people.

[02] The official language of the Czech Republic is Czech and the Czech currency is the Czech crown (code: CZK[1]).

[03] Because of its strategic position in the heart of Europe, the Czech Republic has one of the densest railway networks in Europe (9 505 kilometres of track). The road network in the Czech Republic is 55 653 kilometres long. The country's main international airport is Václav Havel Airport in Prague. Other airports providing international air services are in Brno, Karlovy Vary, Mošnov (near Ostrava), Pardubice and Kunovice (near Uherské Hradiště).

[04] One of the main attractions of the Czech economy is its skilled and well-educated workers, who can be employed for considerably lower costs than those in western economies. Average gross monthly income was CZK32 466 (approx. EUR1 250) in 2019.

[05] The Czech Republic produces significant quantities of bituminous coal, anthracite, and brown coal. Small quantities of petroleum and natural gas are produced, too. The Czech Republic has limited deposits of metal ores (lead and zinc ores, tin). Other resources include uranium, graphite, clay and kaolin.

Historical Background

[06] The recent history of the Czech Republic began in 1918, when the Republic of Czechoslovakia was formed. After 1933, Czechoslovakia remained the only democracy in Central and Eastern Europe. Czechoslovakia fell under German occupation during World War II. The Communist Party's influence rose strongly during those years thanks to its resistance activities. As a result, Czechoslovakia became a single-party communist state under Soviet influence in 1948. The reform movement known as the 'Prague Spring' was suppressed by the Warsaw Pact armies' invasion in 1968, and Czechoslovakia was occupied until the 1989 Velvet Revolution, when the communist regime collapsed. On 1 January 1993, Czechoslovakia split into the

[1] On 30 Jun. 2019 the exchange rate was app. EUR1 = CZK26; USD1 = CZK22; GBP1 = CZK28.

Czech Republic and the Slovak Republic, which became separate, independent states.

[07] Since the Velvet Revolution, the Czech Republic has gone through extensive economic reforms, including extensive privatisation (which helped to create a dynamic and modern economy). The Czech Republic has also become a member of many important international organisations, in particular, the Organisation for Economic Co-operation and Development (OECD) in 1995, The North Atlantic Treaty Organisation in 1999 and the European Union in 2004. Since 2007, the Czech Republic has formed a part of the Schengen Area.

Legal System

[08] The Czech legal system is based on the civil law system, in particular, the Germanic branch of civil law. The legal system is based on written sources of law, namely acts (adopted by the Parliament), delegated legislation (adopted by government or ministries), ratified international treaties, and EU law. Most of the areas of the legal system are systematically codified (e.g., in the Civil Code, Criminal Code, Administrative Code).

[09] Business people and legal practitioners who are used to working in civil law jurisdictions will not feel ill at ease with the structure of commercial law in the Czech Republic. There are certainly many features in the Czech legal system that are particular to this country, but the framework will be familiar. These features and the system itself will seem quite different to business people and lawyers accustomed to a common law environment.

[10] In many respects, the Czech legal environment is liberal, with few impediments to, and legislated protection of, foreign investment.

[11] The Czech Republic ranked 35th out of 190 countries in the World Bank Ease of Doing Business Economy Rankings in 2018.

[12] The Czech Republic has a completely new system of private law. The new Civil Code and the new Business Corporations Act became effective on 1 January 2014. The new laws draw their inspiration from the pre-World War II legal tradition and the Austrian, French, German, Italian, Quebec and Swiss civil codes. Many of the changes brought by the new legislation should have a positive effect on M&A activities in the Czech Republic. For more details, *see* paragraphs [16]–[24] below.

Cultural Aspects

[13] In general, the Czech Republic is open to foreign investments. As described in paragraphs [08]–[12], the Czech legal environment is rather liberal.

[14] The Czech Republic is not an expensive place to do business, but there are regional differences (i.e., Prague is significantly more expensive than other regions where the costs of workforce, premises, etc. are lower).

[15] Given that the Czech Republic is fully part of Western culture, there are no local business practices or cultural issues which should represent a hurdle to a foreign investor. While giving and accepting gifts is not a normal feature of business transactions, a certain reasonable amount of hospitality is common (e.g., client receptions and small Christmas gifts).

THE REGULATORY FRAMEWORK

New Czech Private Law

[16] The new Civil Code and the new Business Corporations Act became effective on 1 January 2014, replacing the Commercial Code and the old Civil Code.

[17] The new laws completely changed the Czech legal landscape and brought, *inter alia*, the following revolutionary changes. The new laws:

- emphasise the principle that contracts should be performed and significantly limit the reasons for the invalidity of contracts. In most cases, even if there is a reason for a contract to be declared invalid, it will be declared invalid only if a party to the agreement challenges it; otherwise it will be deemed valid;
- recognise the concept of a 'trust' as an organisational separation of property which does not lead to the establishment of a separate legal entity;
- cancel section 196a of the Commercial Code, which governed the terms under which transactions between related parties may have been carried out – due to its vague wording, section 196a was often breached and was the single most important reason for the invalidity of contracts under Czech law;
- restore the principle that was valid in Czechoslovakia until 1950 that a building is from a legal point of view a part of the plot of land on which it is built;
- eliminate and unify the dual regulation of contracts and obligations that were contained in both the old Civil Code and the old Commercial Code and now is contained only in the Civil Code; and
- cancel the Act on Lease and Sub-lease of Non-residential Premises. The strictness of the terms set out by this act (which had to be complied with for any lease agreement to be valid) was the most common reason for the invalidity of lease agreements of non-residential premises.

[18] In the area of corporate law, they have:

- introduced greater freedom and flexibility for shareholders to regulate their relationship and tailor their rights and obligations in relation to themselves and their companies. For example, a limited liability company may have different types of ownership interests which differ in terms of the rights and obligations that are attached to them, while a joint-stock company may issue different types of shares with different rights attached to them;

- permitted a company to pay a deposit dividend;
- allowed a joint-stock company to have a single-tier board;
- introduced the obligation for all joint-stock companies to have a website;
- cancelled the obligation for limited liability companies and joint-stock companies to have a reserve fund;
- decreased the minimum amount of registered capital for a limited liability company from approximately EUR6 700 to approximately EUR0.03 per member (e.g., the minimum amount of registered capital required for a limited liability company with two members is EUR0.06); and
- speeded up the registration of corporate changes in the Commercial Register and allowed for direct registration of such changes in the Commercial Register by Czech notaries.

[19] The Business Corporations Act gives existing companies founded under the old Commercial Code the choice of remaining governed by the current regulations of the Commercial Code or opting into the Business Corporations Act.

[20] The Business Corporations Act introduces a new and untested legal regime. Nevertheless, there are convincing arguments for existing companies to opt into the Business Corporations Act.

[21] Even if an existing company decides not to opt into the Business Corporations Act as a whole, those provisions in its existing founding documents which do not conform to the mandatory provisions of the Business Corporations Act became void on 1 January 2014. Furthermore, existing companies also had an obligation to modify such documents so that they comply with the mandatory provisions of the Business Corporations Act and deposit them with the Czech Commercial Register by 30 June 2014.

[22] The Business Corporations Act does not state which of its provisions are mandatory. Consequently, it is in many cases unclear whether a particular provision of the Business Corporations Act is mandatory or whether companies are able to regulate a specific issue otherwise.

[23] Unless a company adopts the Business Corporations Act regime, there is a risk that the company will not be clear about which provisions of its founding documents are valid and which rules it must follow. In addition, if a company misjudges whether a Business Corporations Act provision is mandatory or not, it may be exposed to legal consequences that will often be unpredictable. The difficulty of predicting the extent of these consequences is compounded by the fact that it may very well take years before the case law of the courts becomes unified and the status of certain provisions is fully clarified.

[24] On the other hand, if a company does adopt the Business Corporations Act as a whole, it can eliminate the aforementioned risk by adopting new founding documents. These documents could then be structured so that they differ from the statutory provisions of the Business Corporations Act only when this is explicitly allowed by the Business Corporations Act.

Available Corporate Structures

[25] Business in the Czech Republic is conducted by a variety of different entrepreneurial entities. These include entrepreneurs carrying out business alone (sole traders) and the following types of companies: limited liability companies (*společnost s ručením omezeným* or s.r.o.), joint-stock companies (*akciová společnost* or a.s.), general commercial partnerships (*veřejná obchodní společnost* or v.o.s.) and limited partnerships (*komanditní společnost* or k.s.). Cooperatives also exist as a special legal form. Foreign entities can register to conduct business in the Czech Republic via a branch or participation in Czech entities under the same conditions as the Czech entities. In addition, the following European forms of legal entities are allowed to operate in the Czech Republic (i) a European Economic Interest Grouping, (ii) a European Company (Societas Europea), and (iii) a European Cooperative Society.

Commercial Register

[26] All companies and cooperatives are legal entities and are registered in the Commercial Register kept by the Regional Courts of the region in which the company has its registered seat (the '*Commercial Register*'). The registration and any subsequent changes to the registered information may be made in the Commercial Register both by the court or, if conditions set out by the law are met, by a notary. Registration by a notary is cheaper and faster than registration by the court.

[27] In principle, if a third party relies on the information entered in the Commercial Register, it is protected against the company in the event the information in the Commercial Register is proved untrue.

[28] The Commercial Register is accessible over the Internet on www.justice.cz. Although the Commercial Register is still the primary point of contact if one wishes to obtain an original extract (hard copy) from the Commercial Register, it is also possible to obtain the extract from a notary or at Czech Point offices (www.czechpoint.cz).

[29] The Commercial Register maintains a collection of documents in which the important corporate documents, such as founding deeds, memoranda of association, articles of association and financial statements, are deposited (the '*Collection of Documents*'). Documents deposited there are accessible to the public. Certain documents may only be filed with the Commercial Register in electronic form.

[30] Certain types of documents that are to be submitted to the Commercial Register and the Collection of Documents must be executed in Czech (e.g., a merger project, a memorandum of association of a joint-stock company or a limited liability company).

[31] Other types of documents may be executed in a foreign language and translated into Czech by a Czech sworn translator. If such documents are executed in an official language of any Member State of the European Union or the European Economic Area, a plain translation is sufficient.

[32] The court maintaining the Commercial Register may also declare that it does not require certain types of documents to be translated for filing and registration purposes.

Data Mailboxes

[33] On 1 November 2009, the Czech Republic implemented a system for the official electronic delivery of documents (i) between public authorities, (ii) from public authorities to legal entities, (iii) from public authorities to certain individuals and (iv) from individuals to public authorities.

[34] A data mailbox is an electronic storage space similar to an e-mail account which has been set up and is operated by the state.

[35] All legal entities (including all Czech companies) and public authorities are required by law to have data mailboxes. Individuals may also have data mailboxes but are not required by law to have them. Certain business professionals, such as insolvency trustees, tax advisers and attorneys, are required by law to have data mailboxes.

[36] All documents sent by public authorities to legal entities or to individuals who have data mailboxes must be sent to a data mailbox – i.e., they must be sent in electronic form rather than by post.

[37] Messages delivered to a data mailbox are deemed delivered when the authorised user of the mailbox logs into the data mailbox. If the authorised entity does not log into the data mailbox, a message is deemed to have been delivered after a lapse of ten days, starting on the day on which the message was delivered to the data mailbox.

Common Transactions

[38] Within the context of corporate mergers and acquisitions, it is primarily limited liability companies and joint-stock companies that are involved. Both are equity-based and have registered capital that is contributed by their founders. They are both distinct legal entities, and the financial liability of their shareholders is limited.

[39] Generally, both individuals and legal entities may enter into joint venture agreements, become a partner in a general commercial partnership, limited partnership or silent partnership, or become a shareholder in a limited liability or joint-stock company. As far as sole ownership is concerned, generally both a limited liability company and a joint-stock company may have a sole owner and both may

be the sole owner of another company. Thus, for example, a limited liability company may become the sole shareholder of a joint-stock company or vice versa. Other types of entrepreneurial entities may also become the sole owner of a joint-stock company or a limited liability company. Furthermore, two or more companies may be merged or consolidated into one company without liquidation of the companies.

Comparison of Limited Liability Company and Joint-Stock Company

	Limited Liability Company	*Joint-Stock Company*
Basic characteristics	A limited liability company (in *Czech: 'společnost s ručením omezeným'* or *'s.r.o.' or 'spol. s r.o.*) is the vehicle generally preferred by enterprises with a limited number of investors who plan to hold their investments in the company for the mid- to long term. A limited liability company is typically used by small- to medium-sized enterprises.	A joint-stock company (in Czech: *'akciová společnost' or 'a.s.')* is the vehicle generally preferred by large enterprises and by enterprises who want to be listed on a stock exchange.
Founding	A limited liability company may be founded by one or more legal entities and by one or more individuals, or by a combination of individuals and legal entities.	A joint-stock company may be founded by one or more legal entities and by one or more individuals, or by a combination of individuals and legal entities.
	A limited liability company may have an unlimited number of founders and an unlimited number of shareholders.	A joint-stock company may have an unlimited number of founders and an unlimited number of shareholders.

	Limited Liability Company	*Joint-Stock Company*
	The founders establish a company by means of executing a memorandum of association or, in the case of a sole shareholder, a founding deed – both in the form of a notarial deed.	The founders or a sole founder establishes the company with the execution of the articles of association in the form of a notarial deed.
	The company is created by its registration in the Commercial Register.	The company is created by its registration in the Commercial Register.
	Members of a limited liability company are registered in the Commercial Register.	Shareholders of a joint-stock company are not registered in the Commercial Register. However, if a joint-stock company has only one shareholder, it must be registered in the Commercial Register.
	The ban on chaining of limited liability companies was cancelled from 1 January 2014 (i.e., a limited liability company with a sole shareholder may, from that date, be the sole founder or the sole shareholder of another limited liability company).	The chaining of joint-stock companies has never been prohibited (i.e., a joint-stock company with a sole shareholder may be the sole founder or the sole shareholder of another joint-stock company).
Registered capital	The registered capital of a limited liability company is composed of the contributions made by its shareholders. The minimum contribution of each shareholder to the registered capital is CZK1.	The registered capital of a joint-stock company is divided into a certain number of shares. The minimum registered capital of a joint-stock company is CZK2 million. It is also possible to issue shares without a nominal value or with different values.

	Limited Liability Company	*Joint-Stock Company*
	Contributions to the registered capital of a limited liability company can be financial or in-kind.	Contributions to the registered capital of a joint-stock company can be financial or in-kind.
	The entire amount of the contribution premium, if applicable, and at least 30% of subscribed monetary contributions must be paid up before the filing of an application for the registration of the company in the Commercial Register.	The entire amount of the share premium, if applicable, and at least 30% of the nominal or accounting value of the subscribed shares must be paid up before the filing of an application for the registration of the company in the Commercial Register.
	Non-monetary contributions must be made before the company's registration in the Commercial Register.	Non-monetary contributions must be made before the company's registration in the Commercial Register.
	A memorandum of association can stipulate that the shareholders have an obligation to make additional contributions outside the registered capital of the company. The size of such mandatory contributions is not limited by the Business Corporations Act. The shareholders can stipulate such limitation in the memorandum of association. To protect shareholders against unreasonable mandatory contributions, the Business Corporations Act introduces the right of any shareholder who did not agree to the mandatory	Unlike in the case of the regulation of a limited liability company, contributions 'outside of the registered capital' are only voluntary and the duty to contribute may not be imposed on the shareholders. Such contributions can be made and are, in principle, based on an agreement between the shareholder and the company. It is, therefore, advisable to regulate the issue of contributions to the other capital funds in a joint-stock company in the company's articles of association.

	Limited Liability Company	*Joint-Stock Company*
	contribution to exit the company. This right, however, may be excluded in the memorandum of association.	
Memorandum of Association (Limited Liability Company) **Articles of Association (Joint-stock Company)**	The regulation of a limited liability company is quite liberal and gives shareholders great freedom to change their rights and obligations vis-à-vis each other and the company.	The regulation of a joint-stock company is quite liberal and gives shareholders great freedom to change their rights and obligations vis-à-vis each other and the company.
	The Business Corporations Act allows for tens of deviations from the default wording of the law in areas relating for example to: – types of ownership interest in the company; – rights and obligations attached to an ownership interest in the company; – transferability of ownership interests in the company; – types of securities issued by the company; – conflicts of interest; – voting rights; – financial assistance; – distribution of profits – e.g., to whom it may be paid out;	The Business Corporations Act allows for tens of deviations from the default wording of the law in areas relating for example to: – classes / types of shares; – rights attached to shares; – transferability of shares; – types of securities issued by the company; – conflicts of interest; – voting rights; – financial assistance; – distribution of profit – to whom it may be paid out, fixed share, subordinated share, calculation of the share other than by reference to a share in the registered capital; – publication of accounts;

	Limited Liability Company	*Joint-Stock Company*
	– general meeting – convening, per rollam decisions, quorums and required voting majorities, powers of the general meeting; – directors – number of directors, duration of their office, substitutes, requirement for directors to act jointly in order for their acts to be binding for the company; – custodian of the company; – information duties of the management; and – contributions to other capital funds of the company. As the shareholders may agree in the memorandum of association on additional duties of a holder of a particular share in the company that pass with the transfer of that share to the buyer (including, for example, a duty to provide additional funds to the company), it is essential that a purchaser's due diligence includes a thorough review of the memorandum of association.	– general meeting – convening, per rollam decisions, quorums and required majorities of votes, powers of the general meeting; – board of directors – number of directors, duration of their office, substitutes, requirement for directors to act jointly for their acts to be binding for the company; – custodian of the company; – information contained in the register of shareholders; and – management structure of the company.

	Limited Liability Company	*Joint-Stock Company*
Ownership interest **Shares**	A limited liability company does not issue shares. The ownership interest represents the shareholder's participation in the company and the rights and duties derived from such participation. The size of the ownership interest is determined by the ratio of a particular shareholder's investment contribution to the company's registered capital (unless the memorandum of association provides otherwise). An ownership interest can also be represented by a certificated security called a 'common certificate' (in Czech: '*kmenový list*'). The issuance of such security is possible only in respect of ownership interests whose transfer is not restricted or conditional. A common certificate can be transferred by means of an oral/written agreement, an endorsement and a handover of the common certificate.	A joint-stock company may have: – bearer shares–only in immobilised form (i.e., physically deposited in a bank) or in a book-entered form (i.e., registered in the Central Securities Depository[2]). Certificated bearer shares were prohibited with effect from 1 January 2014; and – registered shares (issued to a named shareholder) in certificated or book-entered form. In addition, certificated shares may be issued in the form of global share certificates replacing a certain number of certificated shares which would otherwise need to be issued.

[2] Central Securities Depository keeps records of all book-entered securities issued in the Czech Republic. It is operated by UNIVYC, a.s., which is a subsidiary of the Prague Stock Exchange.

	Limited Liability Company	*Joint-Stock Company*
		From 1 January 2014, certificated bearer shares transformed into registered certificated shares by operation of law unless a company had the bearer shares either: – immobilised (physically deposited) in a bank; or – book-entered in the Central Securities Depository by 31 December 2013.
	An ownership interest in a limited liability company is not as easily transferable as shares in a joint-stock company. It requires a written agreement (with notarised signatures). A shareholder may transfer his ownership interest to another shareholder without the approval of the general meeting (unless the memorandum of association stipulates otherwise). A shareholder may also transfer his ownership interest to a third party with the approval of the general meeting (unless the memorandum of association stipulates that such approval is not required).	If a company did not take any action by 31 December 2013 and its shares were transformed into registered certificated shares by operation of law, there were additional important deadlines relating to the abovementioned transformation: – A company was obliged to request its shareholders to present their shares to the company either for their exchange or for recording the required information on the shares by 30 March 2014; – Shareholders had to surrender their shares to the company (in order to comply with the abovementioned duty) by 30 June 2014;

	Limited Liability Company	*Joint-Stock Company*
		– The board of directors was required to file the new wording of the articles of association and to record the change of the form of the shares in the Commercial Register by 30 June 2014; and – Each shareholder holding registered certificated shares must provide the company with the number of its bank account by the date of the first general meeting held after 30 June 2013. All payments made by the company to such shareholders in connection with their holding shares in the company are to be made to this bank account. The bank account number will be recorded in the shareholders' register maintained by the company. If the shareholders did not surrender their shares within the above-mentioned time period they lost all rights pertaining to the shares until they comply with the above-mentioned obligations.

	Limited Liability Company	*Joint-Stock Company*
	From 1 January 2014, a limited liability company may have more than one type of ownership interest, to which different rights and obligations attach. For example, the obligation to work for the company can attach to one ownership interest and the obligation to contribute a higher sum of capital to the company can attach to another one. A shareholder may hold more than one ownership interest (provided that the memorandum of association so allows).	Under the old Commercial Code, a joint-stock company could only issue common shares and priority shares. This limitation has been abolished by the Business Corporations Act. A joint-stock company may now issue various types of shares, to which different rights attach. The difference between various classes of shares could lie, for example, in each class of shares having a different share in profits; alternatively, shares of a particular class could incorporate multiple voting rights. It is not clear under Czech law whether the rights attached to the shares must be somehow related to the corporate matters of the company or whether a share could incorporate, for example, a right to a discount in the issuer's company store or a right to a free parking in a certain location owned by the issuer. However, to all types of shares issued by the company identical obligations must attach.
Corporate bodies	The corporate governance of a limited liability company is simpler than that of a joint-stock company.	The corporate governance of a joint-stock company is more complex than that of a limited liability company.

	Limited Liability Company	*Joint-Stock Company*
		There are two possible corporate structures for a joint-stock company: (i) a dualistic structure (with board of directors and supervisory board), and (ii) a monistic structure (with a single director and an administrative board). The choice of the corporate structure must be stipulated in the articles of association. As the option to have a monistic structure was introduced from 1 January 2014, most of the joint-stock companies in the Czech Republic have a dualistic management structure.
	Corporate Structure The executive body of a limited liability company is made up of one or more executive directors. Executive directors are appointed and recalled by the general meeting. The law does not require a limited liability company to establish a supervisory board; however, a supervisory board can be established, provided that the memorandum of association so stipulates.	**Corporate Structure – Dualistic** The executive body of a joint-stock company is the board of directors. Members of the board of directors are appointed and recalled by the general meeting (or by the supervisory board if the articles of association so stipulate). The board of directors has three members, unless the articles of association stipulate a different number of members; the minimal number is one.

	Limited Liability Company	*Joint-Stock Company*
		A joint-stock company with a dualistic management structure must have a supervisory board, which is obliged to oversee the manner in which the board of directors exercises its powers and the manner in which the business of the joint-stock company is conducted. For this purpose, it has the right to examine all the records and documents of the joint-stock company (including the financial statements and minutes of the board of directors), to convene a general meeting of shareholders under certain circumstances, and to represent the joint-stock company in actions against members of the board of directors. The members of a supervisory board must act with the care of a diligent manager. The supervisory board has three members, unless the articles of association stipulate a different number of members; the minimum number is one. The supervisory board reviews the annual, extraordinary and consolidated financial accounts, and, if applicable, interim financial accounts and proposals for profit distribution and coverage of losses, and submits its comments to the general meeting.

	Limited Liability Company	Joint-Stock Company
		The supervisory board is entitled to convene a general meeting, if the interests of the company so require. The Business Corporations Act originally did not require joint-stock companies to have employee representatives elected as members of the supervisory board. An amendment to the Business Corporations Act passed in 2016, however, reintroduced this requirement and stipulated that companies with more than 500 employees must by 14 January 2019 have at least a third of the members of the supervisory board elected by employees. **Corporate Structure–Monistic** Alternatively, instead of a board of directors and a supervisory board, a joint-stock company may have an administrative board and a statutory director. The main advantage of this structure is that one person may manage a joint-stock company (if a single statutory director is also a chairman of the administrative board).

Limited Liability Company	*Joint-Stock Company*
	The prevailing view among leading legal scholars is that the requirement to have at least one-third of the members of the supervisory board elected by employees does not apply to companies with monistic corporate structure (i.e., one-third of the members of the administrative board does not have to be elected by employees). **Other corporate bodies – Monistic / Dualistic Structure:** Entities of public interest (i.e., in particular, Czech legal entities whose securities have been accepted for trading on regulated markets, banks, insurance and reinsurance companies, pension funds, savings and credit cooperatives, investment firms, investment companies, investment funds and commercial companies or cooperatives or consolidated accounting units, if the average converted number of employees of such companies or units has exceeded 4 000 people during the previous accounting period) have a duty to establish an audit committee as another mandatory body of a joint-stock company.

	Limited Liability Company	Joint-Stock Company
		The members of the audit committee are appointed by the general meeting. The audit committee must have at least three members. The majority of the members of that committee must be independent and must have at least three years of practical experience in accounting or statutory audits. The audit committee shall, in particular, (i) follow the procedures for compiling annual accounts and consolidated annual accounts; (ii) follow the efficiency of internal controls in the company, internal audit, and/or the systems of risk management; (iii) follow the process of statutory auditing of the annual accounts and consolidated annual accounts; (iv) assess the independence of statutory auditors and audit firms and, in particular, the provision of auxiliary services to the audited company; and (v) recommend auditors to the supervisory body and justify its recommendation.

	Limited Liability Company	*Joint-Stock Company*
Acting on behalf of a company	Unless the memorandum of association states otherwise, an executive director may independently perform acts of law that are binding on the limited liability company. Information on whether an executive director may act independently or whether the memorandum of association requires executive directors to act jointly must be registered in the Commercial Register. Decisions of the members of the executive body on the business management of a company are taken by a simple majority of votes. A legal entity may also be appointed as an executive director of a limited liability company; however, it is not common.	**Dualistic structure** Unless the articles of association state otherwise, each member of the board of directors may independently perform acts of law that are binding on the joint-stock company. Information on whether a member of the board of directors may act independently or whether the articles of association require members of the board of directors to act jointly must be registered in the Commercial Register. Decisions of the board of directors are taken by a simple majority or another majority specified in the articles of association. The board of directors is a 'collective' body, and its decisions must be recorded in minutes. (b) Monistic structure The statutory director may act independently on behalf of a company. It is not clear under Czech law whether the administrative board can also act on behalf of a company. (c) General A legal entity may also be appointed as a member of the executive body of a joint-stock company; however, it is not common.

	Limited Liability Company	*Joint-Stock Company*
	Executive directors of a company generally may not act on behalf of the company in a capacity other than that of members of the executive body of the company. The exceptions are stipulated by the new Civil Code. If an executive director, is under the founding documents of a company, authorised to act independently on behalf of the company, such director never needs to be authorised by a power of attorney for his acts to be binding on the company. If an executive director, is under the founding documents, required to act jointly with another member of the executive body for his acts to be binding on the company, the new Civil Code stipulates that a company may grant a power of attorney to such director to act independently on behalf of the company only to perform a specifically defined legal act (i.e., not to grant a general power of attorney).	Rules applicable to executive directors of a limited liability company relating to members of the executive body of a limited liability company acting based on a power of attorney and also apply to members of an executive body of a joint-stock company – *See* the left column.

	Limited Liability Company	*Joint-Stock Company*
Duty of care	Members of company bodies must act with the care of a diligent manager and their responsibility cannot be limited or excluded.	Members of company bodies must act with the care of a diligent manager and their responsibility cannot be limited or excluded.
	The Business Corporations Act explicitly codifies a business judgment rule which stipulates that an executive director is not liable for the result of the entrepreneurial activities of a company, but only for ensuring the due and diligent exercise of such activities. This means that even if an executive director's decision causes a loss to the company, he will not be liable if he acted on the basis of sufficient information in the justifiable interests of (and with loyalty to) a company.	The rules applicable to members of company bodies in a limited liability company relating to the duty of care, business judgment, receiving orders from other corporate bodies, the legal relationship of the members of the company bodies with the company, and consequences of a breach of their duties also apply to members of the bodies of a joint-stock company – *See* the left column.
	An executive director may receive an order regarding how to manage the business affairs of a company only in the following two cases: (i) if an executive director requests such an order from a general meeting, or (ii) if an order is given by an executive body of a controlling person to an executive body of a controlled person if both companies belong to an openly declared concern.	

	Limited Liability Company	*Joint-Stock Company*
	An executive director usually performs its duties on the basis of an agreement on the performance of the office of a director. Such agreement must contain a list of all monetary and non-monetary benefits that a director receives from the company and such agreement must be approved by a general meeting. Failure to comply with this statutory requirement results in the director performing the office free of charge and acceptance of any benefits may in this case constitute a crime. A breach of the duty to act with the care of a diligent business person may result in the executive director: – being obliged to pay damages; – being criminally liable for breach of his duties; – being obliged to return any benefits received from the company for the period starting two years before the declaration of the insolvency of the company; – being prohibited by a court from performing activities of an executive director for a period of three years; and	

	Limited Liability Company	*Joint-Stock Company*
	– becoming a guarantor of the debts of the company. Illegal acts of executive directors may also result in criminal liability of the company. For more information about criminal liability of legal entities please *See* paragraphs [210]–[228] (*Other relevant laws, anti-bribery*) below.	
Shareholders' rights	The rights of shareholders in a limited liability company are broadly similar to the rights of shareholders in a joint-stock company – *See* the right column.	Shareholders are entitled at the general meeting to inspect and approve the financial statements of a joint-stock company and the reports prepared by the board of directors and the supervisory board. At the general meeting, shareholders may appoint and recall the members of the board of directors (unless the articles of association stipulate that the supervisory board appoints the members of the board of directors) and the members of the supervisory board. No shareholder is entitled to receive any business-related information from the management of a company other than the reports and other information provided to all shareholders.

	Limited Liability Company	Joint-Stock Company
		Shareholders participate in the profits of the joint-stock company through dividends approved by the general meeting of shareholders. Dividends may only be paid when the general meeting has approved the payment of dividends on the basis of the company's economic performance, as set out in the annual statement. Unlike under the old Commercial Code, the Business Corporations Act allows the making of dividend prepayments (interim dividends) before the general meeting has decided to pay dividends. The interim dividends may be paid out only on the basis of interim financial statements which will confirm that the company has enough funds to distribute profit and in compliance with further rules stipulated by the Business Corporations Act as to which company funds may be used and to what extent. It is important to note that if the final end-of-year results would not make it possible to pay dividends, any interim dividends would have to be returned to the company. Dividends or interim dividends may not be paid out if it would render the company insolvent.

Limited Liability Company	*Joint-Stock Company*
	The Czech Supreme Court's decisions, relating to payment of dividends under the old Commercial Code from which followed that financial statements on the basis of which a general meeting approves the payment of dividends may not be older than six months, are not applicable to payment of dividends under the Business Corporations Act. The prevailing view is that it is possible for a general meeting to approve the payment of dividends under the Business Corporations Act even on the basis of financial statements older than six months; however, the dividend may be paid out only if the payment of the dividends would not cause an insolvency of the company. Further, the right to receive dividends can only be transferred separately after the decision of the general meeting on dividends has been taken. Unlike under the old Commercial Code, a reserve fund is no longer obligatory. Existing companies may dissolve their reserve fund. Minority shareholders holding shares whose total nominal value or number of shares amounts to 3% of the

	Limited Liability Company	Joint-Stock Company
		registered capital (5% in a joint-stock company with a registered capital lower than CZK100 m, 1% in a joint-stock company with a registered capital higher than CZK500 m) may request that the board of directors convene a general meeting with an agenda proposed by the minority shareholders. Each shareholder is also generally entitled to challenge a decision of the general meeting in court. All shareholders have a pre-emptive right under the Business Corporations Act to subscribe to newly issued shares (if the shares are to be subscribed for monetary consideration – i.e., not in the case of in-kind consideration). Such pre-emptive right may not be limited or excluded in the articles of association. The pre-emptive right may be limited or excluded by a decision of the general meeting only on the grounds of an important interest of the company recognised by the general meeting of the joint-stock company.

	Limited Liability Company	*Joint-Stock Company*
Controlling relationship	*See* the right column which also applies to limited liability companies.	Unlike the old Commercial Code, the Business Corporations Act does not regulate controlling agreements and agreements on the transfer of profits. Instead, it distinguishes three levels of control under Czech law: (i) influence, (ii) control, and (iii) concern, and sets out the legal regime governing them. Influence – an influential person is a person who, due to its influence, decisively and significantly influenced acts of a company. Control – a controlling person is a person who may directly or indirectly exercise decisive influence on the company. The law stipulates assumptions under which a person is deemed to be a controlling person. Concern – one or more persons are subjected to uniform control which means an influence exerted by the leader of a concern over the subordinated companies in such concern, such influence being exercised for the purpose of the long-term implementation of the interests of the concern within the uniform concern policy and the systematic management of at least one important part or activity of the concern.

	Limited Liability Company	*Joint-Stock Company*
		Members of the executive body of a company have exclusive authority to manage their company. Such members are required to exercise such authority with the care of a diligent manager and for the commercial benefit of the company they manage. This means that transactions or agreements authorised by them and entered into by their companies must be reasonable and confer upon their company reasonable commercial benefit.
		All persons who by exercising their influence decisively and significantly influence acts of a company to its detriment shall reimburse the company for damage thus caused unless they prove that they in good faith assumed that they acted on the basis of reliable information in the justifiable interest of the influenced person.
		An influential person guarantees by operation of law the settlement of all debts of the influenced person which the influenced person is unable to fully or partially settle due to the influence exercised by the influenced person.

Limited Liability Company	*Joint-Stock Company*
	An exception to this rule is a situation in which a company is part of a declared concern. A declared concern is defined as a situation where one or more persons are subjected to a uniform control by another person or persons belonging to the same concern and the existence of the concern is declared on the web pages of the controlling entity (both Czech and foreign) and the controlled entity (the prevailing view is that this obligation applies only to Czech controlled companies and not foreign companies that are part of the concern). In such a case, members of an executive body must still act with the care of a diligent business person but are not liable for damage if they can prove that they could have justifiably believed that the damage was caused in the interest of the controlling company or another company within the same concern and was or will be settled within the concern. A court may decide on the basis of a petition of an insolvency trustee or a creditor that a member of an executive body of a company or a past member of an executive body of a company guarantees the obligations of the company if:

	Limited Liability Company	*Joint-Stock Company*
		– a company is declared insolvent; and – a member of an executive body or a past member of an executive body of a company knew or should have known that a company was in a situation of threatened 'insolvency' and in breach of its fiduciary duties failed to do everything required and reasonably anticipated to prevent the insolvency of the company. The Business Corporations Act stipulates that this provision also applies to influential and controlling persons. It is currently not clear under Czech law in what circumstances a court could decide (with reference to this statutory provision) that an influential or controlling person guarantees the obligations of the insolvent company. The prevailing interpretation of this provision is that such obligation could be imposed only in extraordinary circumstances, as neither influential persons nor controlling persons have a fiduciary duty towards the respective controlled person and therefore, the basic condition for the application of this provision cannot be met. According to

Limited Liability Company	Joint-Stock Company
	this view, however, a court could create a guarantee obligation on the part of these persons if their influence and actions in relation to the controlled person were so strong and influential that they would be similar to the influence exerted and actions undertaken by a member of an executive body.

[40] Czech law requires that all companies register by 1 January 2019 their beneficial owner in the register of beneficial owners maintained by the court maintaining the Commercial Register. The information from the register of beneficial owners will not be publicly available; however, the list of persons authorised to access the information from the register is quite extensive (e.g., a court for the purposes of court proceedings, tax authorities for the purposes of tax proceedings, all persons complying with their duty to identify the beneficial owner under the AML legislation).

LAWS AFFECTING M&A

Regulatory Framework

[41] In addition to the new Civil Code and the Business Corporations Act, mergers and acquisitions will be affected by the following regulations:

- Act No. 455/1991 Coll., on Trade Licensing, as amended (the '*Trade Licensing Act*').
- Act No. 21/1992 Coll., on Banks, as amended (the '*Banking Act*').
- Act No. 42/1994 Coll., on Pension Funds, as amended (the '*Pension Funds Act*').
- Act No. 427/2011 Coll., on Supplementary Pension Savings (the '*Supplementary Pension Savings Act*').
- Act No. 87/1995 Coll., on Saving and Credit Cooperatives (the '*Act on Saving and Credit Cooperatives*').
- Act No. 284/2009 Coll., on Electronic Money Institutions (the '*Electronic Money Institutions Act*').
- Act No. 15/1998 Coll., on the Supervision of Capital Markets, as amended (the '*SCM Act*').

- Act No. 363/1999 Coll., on Insurance Companies, as amended (the *'Insurance Act'*).
- Act No. 143/2001 Coll., on Protection of Economic Competition (the *'Competition Act'*).
- Act No. 240/2013 Coll., on Investment Companies and Investment Funds (the *'Investment Companies and Investment Funds Act'*).
- Act No. 256/2004 Coll., on Capital Markets (the *'Capital Markets Act'*).
- Act No. 304/2013 Coll., on Public Registers of Legal and Natural Persons.
- Act No. 627/2004 Coll., on European Company.
- Act No. 307/2006 Coll., on European Cooperative Society.
- Act No. 182/2006 Coll., on Insolvency *('Insolvency Act')*.
- Act No. 418/2011 Coll., on Criminal Liability of Legal Entities (*'ACLLE'*).
- Act No. 40/2009 Coll., the Criminal Code.
- Act No. 141/1961 Coll., the Criminal Procedure Code.
- Act No. 125/2008 Coll., on Transformations of Companies and Cooperatives, as amended (the *'Transformations Act'*).
- Act No. 240/2000 Coll., on Crises Management (the *'Crises Management Act'*).
- Act No. 104/2008 Coll., on Takeover Bids, as amended (the *'Takeover Bids Act'*); and
- Act No. 91/2012 Coll., on Private International Law (the *'Private International Law Act')*.

TRANSFORMATIONS

General Framework

[42] Czech law provides a relatively flexible environment for the transformation of companies. It is possible, for example, to merge a joint-stock company with a limited liability company and a general commercial partnership with a limited partnership. The same applies to demergers of companies. Transformation of a company is also possible if its liquidation has already been decided on or if the insolvency proceedings have been initiated or the company has been declared bankrupt. The Czech law also allows for certain cross-border transformations. A transformation may not be possible if a company is investigated under ACLLE, the Criminal Code and the Criminal Procedure Code.

[43] The legal framework for transformations is the Transformations Act which incorporates the respective European legislation.

[44] The following types of transformations are possible in the Czech Republic:

(i) merger by acquisition or by consolidation (i.e., by formation of a new company);
(ii) cross-border merger by acquisition or by consolidation;
(iii) transfer of business assets to the main shareholder;
(iv) cross-border transfer of business assets to the main shareholder;

(v) demerger by acquisition or by the formation of a new company or by a combination of both methods;
(vi) demerger by spin-off acquisition or with the formation of a new company or by a combination of both methods;
(vii) cross-border demerger;
(viii) transformation of a company's legal form; and
(ix) cross-border change of the registered seat of a company.

Mergers

Merger by Acquisition

[45] In the event of a merger by acquisition, one or more companies are dissolved without liquidation and their business assets, including all rights and obligations, are transferred to one of the companies involved in the merger (the successor company). In principle, shareholders of the dissolving companies become shareholders in the successor company. Their shareholding in the successor company is determined by the proportion of the asset value of their shareholdings in the dissolving companies to the net asset value of the successor company.

Merger by Consolidation

[46] In contrast, in a merger by consolidation, two or more companies are dissolved without liquidation, and their business assets, including all rights and obligations, are transferred to a newly established company. In principle, shareholders of the dissolving companies become shareholders in the newly established company.

Cross-Border Transformations

[47] Under the Transformations Act, the majority of the domestic transformations can also be carried out on a cross-border basis (i.e., the Transformations Act allows for a cross-border merger, cross-border demerger, cross-border transfer of business to the majority shareholder). Moreover, a company can change its legal form in the process of the cross-border change of the registered seat of a company.

Transfer of Business to the Majority Shareholder

[48] If a shareholder owns a certain amount of shares in a company (e.g., in the case of a joint-stock company, shares with a nominal value corresponding to at least 90% of the registered capital and representing at least 90% of the voting rights) (a 'main shareholder'), such shareholder can adopt a decision at the general meeting that the company (the 'target company') be wound up without liquidation and that the target company's business assets be taken over by the main shareholder on the basis of a takeover project.

[49] The results of such a procedure are as follows:

(i) the target company is wound-up without liquidation;
(ii) all of the target company's minority shareholders are 'squeezed-out' and receive compensation; and
(iii) the main shareholder acquires all of the target company's business assets and becomes its legal successor.

[50] As follows from the above, the main shareholder will not acquire all of the target company's shares (i.e., it will not become a 100% shareholder of the target company). Rather, the main shareholder will acquire the business assets and thus become the target company's legal successor, and at the same time, the company will cease to exist. In addition, to carry on the business activities, the main shareholder will need to apply for the relevant trade licence or other licences that were originally held by the target company.

Demerger

Concept of Demerger under Czech Law

[51] There are two types of demergers under Czech law:

(i) demerger by splitting (where the demerged entity ceases to exist) which includes:
  (a) demerger by splitting where the property (assets and liabilities) of the demerged company is transferred to newly established companies;
  (b) demerger by splitting where the property (assets and liabilities) of the demerged company is transferred to already existing successor companies;
  (c) a combination of methods described under (a) and (b) above.
(ii) demerger by spin-off (where the demerged entity survives the demerger) which includes:
  (a) demerger by spin-off where part of the property (assets and liabilities) of the demerged company is transferred to newly established companies;
  (b) demerger by spin-off where part of the property (assets and liabilities) of the demerged company is transferred to already existing successor companies, and
  (c) a combination of methods described under (a) and (b) above.

[52] In the demergers by splitting, a company being split up ceases to exist without liquidation and its business assets, including all rights and obligations, are transferred to the successor companies. In principle, shareholders of the dissolving company become shareholders in the successor companies. Their shareholding is equal to the ratio of participation in the asset value derived from their shareholding in the dissolved company compared to the net asset value of the successor entities. Shareholders may become shareholders in all of the successor companies or just in selected ones.

[53] In the demergers by spin-off, the demerged entity survives the demerger. The procedures for demerger by a spin-off are almost the same as demergers by splitting, and the same legal regulations apply. The Transformations Act also includes provisions on how to deal with uncertainties or doubts on whether an asset or liability has been included in the transferred part of the property or, in the event of more than one successor company, to which company they have actually been transferred. In the first case, the principal rule is that, if in doubt, the asset or liability in question has not been transferred to the successor company but remains with the demerged one. In the latter case, the successor companies become co-owners of the asset and co-debtors of the liability in question.

Transformation of a Legal Form

[54] Under Czech law, it is possible to transform a company's legal form to another without liquidation. The company with the new legal form remains the same legal entity as prior to the transformation, i.e., it is not dissolved. The transformation of the legal form of a company requires registration in the Commercial Register. The procedures as well as the permitted legal form to which a company may be transformed depend on the type of company being transformed.

RELEVANT REGULATORY AUTHORITIES

[55] Under Act No. 6/1993 Coll., on the Czech National Bank, the Czech National Bank (the '*CNB*') is a supervisory authority of the financial market in the Czech Republic. The CNB therefore supervises the banking sector, the capital market, the insurance industry, pension funds, credit unions, bureaux-de-change and payment system institutions. The CNB lays down rules safeguarding the stability of the banking sector, the capital market, the insurance industry and the pension scheme industry. It systematically regulates, supervises and, where appropriate, issues penalties for non-compliance with these rules.

[56] The Office for the Protection of Competition is the central authority of state administration responsible for creating conditions that favour and protect competition, supervision of public procurement, and consultation and monitoring in relation to the provision of state aid.

[57] The timing of the granting of various forms of government approvals and the timing of action undertaken by government bodies – regulatory authorities are in most cases governed by the appropriate laws. In some cases, it is possible to engage with regulatory authorities and their staff personally (i.e., via telephone or e-mail);

in other cases, the regulatory authorities stick to the formal procedures (e.g., regarding the filing of official forms for regulatory inquiries).

CONTROLS/RESTRICTIONS ON FOREIGN INVESTMENT

[58] In general, Czech law provides for the equal rights and obligations of both Czech and foreign legal entities. However, in certain circumstances foreign legal entities are subject to laws and regulations over and above those imposed on Czech legal entities.

Exchange Control

[59] The Czech law, in principle, does not limit payments of capital to and from the Czech Republic. There are no restrictions on Czech legal entities or individuals having their bank accounts abroad.

[60] Under the Crises Management Act, the Czech government may declare a state of emergency in foreign exchange management. During a state of emergency, financial operations between the Czech Republic and foreign countries may be restricted (e.g., deposits of funds abroad and payment operations to and from abroad). However, such restrictions may be imposed only in exceptional situations; to date, no such restrictions have been imposed, and none are expected in the future.

Acquisition of Real Estate by Foreigners

[61] The amendment to the Foreign Exchange Act, which became effective on 19 July 2011, repealed the section of the act that contained rules restricting foreigners' rights to acquire agricultural land and forests in the Czech Republic.

[62] The EU prohibits restrictions on the acquisition of real estate in its Member States as this would be in breach of its rules prohibiting discrimination based on a person's nationality and its rules on the free movement of capital.

[63] However, before joining the EU, the Czech Republic agreed with the EU on two transitional periods during which it could impose restrictions on the acquisition of real estate by foreigners.

[64] The first transitional period applied to all types of real estate other than agricultural land and forests. It expired on 1 May 2009. Since that date all foreigners have been able to acquire all types of real estate in the Czech Republic other than agricultural land and forests.

[65] The second transitional period applied to agricultural land and forests. It expired on 1 May 2011. Consequently, the adoption of the amendment was simply a formal step that was necessary to bring Czech law into compliance with EU law (although even without the amendment the restriction would still not have been applicable, due to the direct application of EU law).

[66] Consequently, all foreigners (irrespective of whether legal entities or individuals) may now acquire any type of real estate in the Czech Republic from a private person directly and not necessarily through establishing a Czech company which would then acquire the real estate (as was usual in the past two decades).

ACQUISITION OF REGULATED ENTITIES

[67] The acquisition by an entity or entities acting in concert of a 'qualified shareholding' or shares above certain thresholds in a regulated entity is conditional upon obtaining prior approval from the relevant regulatory authority. A qualified shareholding means a direct or indirect shareholding which (a) represents 10% or more of the capital or voting rights; or (b) enables the exercise of significant influence over the management of the acquired entity.

[68] Failure to obtain approval does not invalidate the sale, but usually leads to some form of suspension of voting rights.

Banks

[69] Under the Banking Act, the direct or indirect acquisition by an entity or entities acting in concert of the qualified shareholding (as defined in paragraph [67]) in a bank is subject to the prior approval of the CNB. The same applies if an entity or entities acting in concert intend to increase their direct or indirect shareholding above 20%, 30% or 50% of the voting rights or share capital or become the controlling entity of the bank. The approval of the CNB is required even if the voting rights are not exercised.

[70] Under exceptional circumstances the consent may be granted after the threshold is reached/exceeded.

[71] A share acquisition made without the prior approval of the CNB is valid. However, in such case voting rights attached to the shares exceeding the applicable threshold cannot be exercised until the CNB grants its consent. In addition, the CNB may, by its decision delivered in administrative proceedings, suspend certain other shareholder's rights.

[72] If an entity reduces its share in a bank below the applicable threshold or transfers its qualified interest in a bank, it is obliged to notify the CNB of such transaction.

Investment Firms

[73] Under the Capital Markets Act, the direct or indirect acquisition by an entity or entities acting in concert of the qualified shareholding (as defined in the first paragraph [67] above) in an investment firm is subject to the prior approval of the CNB. The same applies if an entity or entities acting in concert intend to increase their direct or indirect shareholding above 20%, 30% or 50% of the voting rights or share capital or become the controlling entity of the investment firm. The approval of the CNB is required even if the voting rights are not exercised.

[74] A share acquisition made without the prior approval of the CNB is valid. However, in such case voting rights attached to the shares exceeding the applicable threshold cannot be exercised until the CNB grants its consent. In addition, the CNB may, by its decision delivered in administrative proceedings, suspend certain other shareholder's rights.

Central Securities Depository and Organisers of Regulated Markets

[75] Under the Capital Markets Act, the acquisition of shares and voting rights in central depositaries and organisers of regulated markets is subject to the same rules as the acquisition of shares and voting rights in investment firms. For more details, *see* paragraphs **[73]** and **[74]** above.

Management Companies and Investment Funds

[76] Under the Collective Investment Act, the direct or indirect acquisition by an entity or entities acting in concert of the qualified shareholding (as defined in the first paragraphs **[67]–[68]** above) in a management company or an investment fund is subject to the prior approval of the CNB. The same applies if an entity or entities acting in concert intend to increase their direct or indirect shareholding above 20%, 30% or 50% of the voting rights or share capital or become the controlling entity of the management company or the investment fund. The approval of the CNB is required even if the voting rights are not exercised.

[77] A share acquisition made without the prior approval of the CNB is valid. However, in such case voting rights attached to the shares exceeding the applicable threshold cannot be exercised until the CNB grants its consent. In addition, the CNB may, by its decision delivered in administrative proceedings, suspend certain other shareholder's rights.

Pension Bunds

[78] In accordance with the existing pension reform in the Czech Republic the pension funds were required to be transformed into transformed funds effective from 1 January 2013. From that date the transformed funds are required to be held by pension companies.

Pension Companies

[79] Under the Supplementary Pension Saving Act, the direct or indirect acquisition by an entity or entities acting in concert of the qualified shareholding (as defined in the first paragraphs **[67]–[68]** above) in a pension company is subject to the prior approval of the CNB. The same applies if an entity or entities acting in concert intend to increase their direct or indirect shareholding above 20%, 30% or 50% of the voting rights or share capital or become the controlling entity of the pension company. The approval of the CNB is required even if the voting rights are not exercised.

[80] A share acquisition made without the prior approval of the CNB is valid. However, in such case voting rights attached to the shares exceeding the applicable threshold cannot be exercised until the CNB grants its consent.

[81] If an entity reduces its share in a pension company below the applicable threshold or transfers its qualified interest in a pension company, it is obliged to notify the CNB of such transaction.

Insurance/Reinsurance Companies

[82] Under the Insurance Act, the direct or indirect acquisition by an entity or entities acting in concert of the qualified shareholding (as defined in the first paragraphs [67]–[68] above) in an insurance company is subject to the prior approval of the CNB. The same applies if an entity or entities acting in concert intend to increase their direct or indirect shareholding above 20%, 30% or 50% of the voting rights or share capital or become the controlling entity of the insurance company. The approval of the CNB is required even if the voting rights are not exercised.

[83] A share acquisition made without the prior approval of the CNB is valid. However, in such case voting rights attached to the shares exceeding the applicable threshold cannot be exercised until the CNB grants its consent.

[84] If an entity reduces its share in an insurance/reinsurance company below the applicable threshold or transfers its qualified interest in a pension company, it is obliged to notify the CNB of such transaction.

Saving and Credit Cooperatives

[85] Under the Act on Saving and Credit Cooperatives, the direct or indirect acquisition by an entity or entities acting in concert of the qualified shareholding (as defined in the first paragraphs[67]–[68]above) in a saving or credit cooperative is subject to the prior approval of the CNB. The same applies if an entity or entities acting in concert intend to increase their direct or indirect shareholding above 20%, 30% or 50% of the voting rights or share capital or become the controlling entity of the a saving or credit cooperative. The approval of the CNB is required even if the voting rights are not exercised.

[86] A share acquisition made without the prior approval of the CNB is valid. However, in such case voting rights attached to the shares exceeding the applicable threshold cannot be exercised until the CNB grants its consent. In addition, the CNB may, by its decision delivered in administrative proceedings, suspend certain other shareholder's rights.

Electronic Money Institution

[87] Under the Electronic Money Institutions Act, the entity which intends to acquire the qualified interest (as defined in the first paragraphs [67]–[68]above), increase its shareholding above the applicable threshold (20%, 30% or 50%) or become the controlling entity of the electronic money institution must inform the CNB. The CNB may initiate proceedings where it disapproves with such transaction. If the CNB disapproves the transaction, the acquirer may not exercise its shareholder rights with respect to the shares exceeding the applicable threshold.

Other Specific Industries

[88] Generally, there are no other restrictions as to the acquisitions of entities active in specific industries in the Czech Republic. However, certain activities (such as arms dealing) may be rendered only with a licence granted by the Czech Republic's authorities, whereas such licence can only be conferred on entities controlled by Czech based companies/individuals. Any acquisition by a foreign entity of a controlling shareholding could, therefore, lead to withdrawal of such licence.

INCENTIVES FOR FOREIGN INVESTMENT

General Information

[89] Investors who locate their investments in the Czech Republic can obtain aid in the form of investment incentives. Czech and foreign legal entities and natural persons conducting business can apply for investment incentives. Only a legal entity with its registered office in the Czech Republic can be a recipient of investment incentives.

[90] Investment incentives are available not only to investors launching or expanding production, but also to technological centres and strategic service centres.

Current Forms of Investment Incentives

[91]

- Corporate income tax relief for ten years.
- Cash grants for job creation.
- Cash grants for training and retraining up to 50% of training costs.
- Cash grants for purchase of fixed assets up to 10% of eligible costs.

CzechInvest

[92] The main state agency dealing with incentives for foreign investment is CzechInvest. It is an agency of the Ministry of Industry and Trade. It was established in 1992, and the agency contributes to attracting foreign investment and developing domestic companies through its services and development programmes.

[93] CzechInvest is exclusively authorised to file applications for investment incentives with the competent governing bodies and prepares draft offers to grant investment incentives. Its task is also to provide potential investors current data and information on business climate, investment environment and investment opportunities in the Czech Republic.

[94] CzechInvest's services include: full information assistance, tailor-made visits, handling of investment incentives, access to EU structural funds, the identification of potential business property, business infrastructure development, search for potential suppliers/JV/acquisition partners, and care of existing investors.

SPECIFIC ISSUES OF COMPANY/SECURITIES LAW

Financial Assistance

[95] Financial assistance is defined as the granting of an advance payment, a loan or a credit by a company for the purpose of acquiring its shares, and the granting of security by such company for these purposes.

[96] It is currently not clear under Czech law whether the prohibition on the granting of financial assistance applies to financial assistance provided for the purposes of acquiring shares in the parent company. In contrast to the old Commercial Code, the Business Corporations Act does not explicitly prohibit this. It could be argued, however, that providing financial assistance in this form could amount to a circumvention of law and that the aim of the prohibition dictates to apply the prohibition also to provision of financial assistance for the purpose of acquiring shares in the parent company.

[97] The prohibition of financial assistance does not apply to limited partnerships (komanditní společnost) and general partnerships (veřejná obchodní společnost).

[98] In an acquisition financing, the Czech target and its Czech subsidiaries will generally not be able to provide security in relation to the acquisition facility, unless the financial assistance meets the criteria set out by the Business Corporations Act. This will, according to the prevailing view, extend to any acquisition refinancing.

[99] Non-Czech subsidiaries of a Czech target are not subject to this prohibition, but rather, are subject to any financial assistance restrictions in the jurisdiction of the non-Czech subsidiary.

[100] Shares in a Czech target held by an acquirer may be used for securing an acquisition facility without breaching the financial assistance prohibition.

[101] There are several methods used to deal with financial assistance issues.

[102] The most common method of dealing with financial assistance for limited liability companies is the whitewash procedure, for joint-stock companies it is the upstream merger of the Czech target into an acquisition vehicle. It is doubtful whether a downstream merger is also possible; in any case, it is not widely used.

[103] Other possible methods include the payment of dividends by the Czech target or the reduction of the registered capital of the Czech target. The Czech market has seen a few instances of the use of these methods as a means of dealing with financial assistance issues.

Limited Liability Company	*Joint-Stock Company*
Conditions under which financial assistance can be provided are less stringent for limited liability companies. A limited liability company may provide financial assistance even if its memorandum of association does not explicitly permit it.	Conditions under which financial assistance can be provided are more onerous for joint-stock companies. A joint-stock company may provide financial assistance only if its articles of association explicitly permit it.

Limited Liability Company	*Joint-Stock Company*
Unless the memorandum of association provides for other conditions, the following conditions apply to limited liability companies:	Unless the articles of association provide for other conditions, the following conditions apply to joint-stock companies:
(a) financial assistance is provided on an arm's-length basis – with a special consideration being given to the interest rate and security provided to the company giving the financial assistance;	(a) financial assistance is provided on an arm's-length basis – with a special consideration being given to the interest rate and security provided to the company giving the financial assistance;
(b) the provision of financial assistance will not cause the bankruptcy of the company;	(b) the provision of financial assistance will not cause the bankruptcy of the company;
(c) the provision of financial assistance has been approved by the general meeting. Contrary to the rules governing joint-stock companies, the approval does not have to be provided prior to the provision of financial assistance;	(c) prior consent must be given to the provision of financial assistance by the general meeting (a two-thirds majority of votes of present shareholders is required) on the basis of the board of directors' report;
(d) the executive director shall prepare a report: – giving a substantive justification of the provision of financial assistance – including a specification of the company's benefits and the risks arising therefrom; – specifying the conditions under which financial assistance will be provided; – explaining why the provision of financial assistance is not in conflict with the interests of the company;	(d) the board of directors shall prepare a report: – giving a substantive justification of the provision of financial assistance – a specification of the company's benefits and the risks arising therefrom; – specifying the conditions under which financial assistance will be provided, including the price for which shares will be acquired by the recipient of financial assistance; – with conclusions on the examination of financial eligibility; and – explaining why the provision of financial assistance is in the company's interest;

Limited Liability Company	*Joint-Stock Company*
N/A	(e) the board of directors will examine the financial eligibility of the person to which financial assistance is provided; If financial assistance is to be provided to a member of an executive body of the company, a person controlling the company, a member of its executive body or a person acting in concert with any of the previously mentioned persons, then the report under item (e) will be reviewed by a reputable expert who is independent of these entities and who will be appointed by the supervisory board. In his/her report the expert will evaluate the correctness of the board of directors' report and provide an express statement on whether or not the provision of financial assistance is in conflict with the company's interests.
N/A	(f) if shares are purchased in a company using financial assistance provided by the very same company, then the price for which these shares are acquired must be fair;
N/A	(g) the provision of financial assistance shall not cause any decrease in the equity capital below the level of the registered capital, plus funds (which under the articles of association or the law cannot be distributed among the shareholders); the calculation of such potential decrease should take into account any possible decrease in equity caused by the company's acquisition of its own shares; and
N/A	(h) the company will create a special reserve fund in the amount of the provided financial assistance.

Security Interests

General Principles of Czech Security Law

[104]

- The Czech Republic is a typical continental jurisdiction. As far as the concept of security is concerned, it falls into a mixed Franco-Latin/Germanic group.
- As a general rule, security has an accessory nature and there is no security without secured debt. There is a notable exception to this rule: 'a released pledge' – i.e., a pledge that exists even after the full settlement of the debt which it secured and which can be used to secure another debt of the debtor.
- Security documents in respect of assets in the Czech Republic should be governed by Czech law.
- A foreign lender may take security over local immovable property.
- There is no concept of a universal floating charge (i.e., all-encompassing security, which is generically defined and covers all present and future assets) under Czech law. The closest form is arguably the pledge of an enterprise (*zástava závodu*) or of a part of an enterprise or the pledge of a collective thing/set of things (*zástavní právo k věci hromadné/souboru věcí*) in general.

[105] An enterprise is deemed to be constituted by the aggregate of debts and assets which an entrepreneur created and which serve the operation of an enterprise. It is a collective thing (*hromadná věc*). It is not a legal person. Given that an enterprise comprises both assets and liabilities, it can also have a negative value.

[106] It is not recommended to rely solely on the pledge of an enterprise as the only security securing a particular claim. The reason is that even if an enterprise is pledged, the individual assets forming the pledged enterprise will not be subject to the pledge when the asset is sold. This means that if the debtor disposes of them, the secured creditor would have no proprietary right against the individual persons that acquired the assets.

[107] Some banks, however, require the pledge of the enterprise to be given as security. In such case it is necessary to pledge the individual assets forming the enterprise first and then pledge the enterprise itself. If the enterprise was pledged first, the law forbids the pledge of individual assets belonging to the pledged enterprise:

(1) A pledgor and pledgee may from 1 January 2014 agree in the pledge agreement that in the event of the enforcement of the pledge, the pledgee will be entitled, under certain conditions protecting the pledgor, to directly sell the pledged assets or to acquire an ownership title to the pledged assets.
(2) Czech law does not permit secured creditors to appoint receivers or administrators at their sole discretion.
(3) There is no general security register. However, in some cases, the perfection of the security requires the entry of the security into specific registers, for example:

- a mortgage needs to be entered into the Real Estate Register;
- a pledge of an ownership interest in a limited liability company that is not incorporated into a common certificate needs to be entered into the Commercial Register;
- a pledge over moveable assets that is not created by the handing-over of the assets to the pledgee needs to be entered into the notarial register of pledges;
- a pledge of receivables may be entered into a notarial register of pledges.

[108] Some of the registers are publicly accessible and some can be searched upon proving a legitimate interest in doing so.

[109] Czech versions of the security agreements (a signed Czech version or an official translation into Czech) need to be presented to the registration authority in order for the registration to proceed.

[110] From 1 January 2014, a pledge registered in a public register or a notarial register of pledges has priority over an unregistered pledge, even if it was created at a later point in time.

[111] This is especially relevant in the case of a pledge of receivables because a pledge of receivables which was registered in the notarial register of pledges would take priority over a purely contractual pledge of receivables not registered in the notarial register of pledges:

- If a negative pledge undertaking is registered in a public register or a notarial register of pledges with respect to an asset as a proprietary right of the creditor, it is enforceable towards third parties who acquired the asset in breach of such undertaking.
- There are no stamp taxes payable in relation to the facility or the security documents.
- There are fees for registering the security in a public register or notarial register of pledges. With the exception of fees for registering security in the notarial register of pledges, the fees are low.

Completion Formalities

Asset	*Formalities*
Real estate	A written agreement with a notarised signature and the registration of the transfer of an ownership right in the Real Estate Cadastre is required for a transfer of real estate.

Asset	*Formalities*
Share in limited liability company	A written agreement with a notarised signature is required for a transfer of a share in a limited liability company. The transfer is registered in the Commercial Register. From 1 January 2014 it is no longer required to file the transfer agreement in the public Collection of Deeds maintained by the Commercial Register.
Share in limited liability company incorporated into common certificate	An agreement, endorsement and hand-over are required for a transfer of a share in a limited liability company incorporated into a common certificate. The transfer is registered in the Commercial Register. It is not required to file the transfer agreement into the public Collection of Deeds maintained by the Commercial Register.
Certificated registered shares	An agreement, endorsement and hand-over are required for a transfer of certificated registered shares. The transfer is not registered in the Commercial Register unless the company has a sole shareholder. It is not required to file the transfer agreement into the public Collection of Deeds maintained by the Commercial Register.
Book-entered shares	An agreement and the registration of book-entered shares in an owner account maintained by a Central Securities Depository are required for a transfer of book-entered shares. It is not required to file the transfer agreement in the public Collection of Deeds maintained by the Commercial Register.
Enterprise	If the buyer is registered in a public register (e.g., it is a limited liability company or a joint-stock company), the new Civil Code does not clearly stipulate a moment at which a transfer of an enterprise takes effect. The relevant provisions of the legal regulations are in contradiction – a transfer of enterprise becomes effective either when the information about the transfer is published in the Commercial Gazette or when it is published online in the Collection of Deeds of the Commercial Register. A transfer agreement suffices for the transfer of an enterprise if the buyer is not registered in the public register.

Asset	*Formalities*
Movable Property	An agreement is required for transfer of title to movable property to the purchaser. The transfer agreement as such does not need to be in writing, but a written form is recommended.
Receivables	Receivables are transferred by an assignment agreement. Unless agreed otherwise, the debtor's consent to the assignment is not required. Once the assignment is notified to the debtor by the assignor or proven by the assignee, the debtor is able to discharge itself of its obligation only by performing its obligations to the assignee and not to the assignor.
Agreements	If the nature of an agreement allows it and the agreement has not yet been performed, an agreement may be transferred with the consent of the assigned party. If the transferee fails to perform its obligations under the transferred agreement, the assigned party may require the transferor to perform the obligations of the transferee under the agreement. The assigned party must request such performance on the part of the transferor within fifteen days (a) of becoming aware of or (b) from the day when it must have found out about the non-performance on the part of the transferee. Otherwise, the assigned party is liable for damage caused by its failure to observe the fifteen-day period set by the new Civil Code.
Intellectual Property Rights	The transfer of intellectual property rights may require registration in a public register (e.g., trademarks and patents). A company's business name registered in the Commercial Register may not be transferred without the simultaneous transfer of the business to which it relates.
Licences	Licences granted under public law may not generally be transferred. Even if a licence has been issued for the operation of an appliance, the new operator will usually need to apply for a new licence from the relevant authority.

Asset	*Formalities*
Employees	If a significant portion of assets relating to certain business activities that will be newly carried out by the transferee of the assets is transferred, employees attributable to such assets may pass by operation of law to the transferee.

INSOLVENCY

General

[112] In principle, the Insolvency Act recognises the following resolution methods: (i) bankruptcy, (ii) reorganisation (i.e., restructuring) and (iii) the discharging of debts (for consumers only). Further, it includes specific rules for the treatment of insolvent financial institutions (as defined in the Insolvency Act, including banks or insurance providers), due to its effect on a large group of creditors.

[113] As for entrepreneurs, there are two methods of resolving insolvency: reorganisation and bankruptcy.

[114] Bankruptcy is by far the most common method of resolving insolvency in the Czech Republic.

Bankruptcy

Insolvency

[115]

(i) If a company is insolvent, bankruptcy may be declared on the basis of a petition filed by the debtor or a petition filed by one or more creditors. A petition for so-called impending insolvency (in Czech: '*hrozící úpadek*') can only be filed by the debtor.

(ii) An insolvent company and its directors have a duty to file for insolvency under Czech law, and the company and its directors may be liable to the creditors for damage or losses incurred if this duty is breached.

(iii) A company is deemed to be insolvent when (i) it has two or more creditors and its debts have been overdue for more than thirty days and it is unable to pay its debts; or (ii) it is overburdened with debts.
A company is deemed to be unable to pay its debts if (i) it stopped paying significant parts of its monetary obligations, or (ii) if its monetary obligations have been overdue for more than three months, or (iii) if its creditors

cannot satisfy any of their overdue claims by enforcement against the debtor's assets, or (iv) if it fails to comply with a duty imposed on it by a court to provide an overview of its financial situation.
A company is deemed to be able to pay its debts, if it meets the financial criteria set out by the Act on Insolvency and Decree of the Ministry of Justice No. 190/2017 Coll. which in essence means that its 'liquidity gap' (i.e., the difference between the amount of its outstanding debts and its liquid assets) is lower than one-tenth of its outstanding debts over a relevant period.
A company is deemed to be overburdened with debts if it has two or more creditors and its liabilities exceed its assets. When assessing the potential over-indebtedness of the debtor, the insolvency court will take into account further management of the company's assets and business.

(iv) If an insolvency petition is filed by the debtor and the decisive facts are well-documented therein and in the supporting documentation, the decision of the court is straightforward. The court takes no steps to identify creditors, etc. (the debtor proves its insolvency using financial statements).

(v) If an insolvency petition is filed by a creditor, it must be proved to the court that the debtor is insolvent. When filing the petition, the creditor must prove to the court that it has at least one mature receivable against the insolvent company which has not yet been paid and must register its receivable in the insolvency proceedings by filing a receivable registration form with the insolvency court. There is no minimum limit for the amount of the receivable. A creditor that is subject to accountancy regulations must evidence its receivable against the debtor by one of the following means: (i) an acknowledgement of the receivable by the debtor with a notarised signature of the debtor; (ii) a notarial or an execution deed containing a consent of the debtor given to the creditor to enforce the debt; or (iii) a confirmation of an auditor, a court-appointed expert, or a tax advisor that the debt is recorded in the creditors' accounting.

Effects of Commencing Insolvency Proceedings, Decision on Insolvency and Declaration of Bankruptcy

[116] The Insolvency Act defines certain points of the insolvency proceedings with which various far-reaching effects are accompanied. They are as follows: the commencement of insolvency proceedings, the decision on insolvency and the declaration of bankruptcy:

(i) The effects of insolvency proceedings (i.e., from the moment the petition for insolvency is published in the insolvency register by the competent insolvency court) are as follows:
   - claims and other rights concerning the estate cannot be enforced outside the insolvency proceedings (i.e., by enforcement/execution in courts);
   - security over the debtor's assets can only be enforced or newly created to the extent permitted under Czech insolvency law;

- the company must refrain from taking any action which would impair the value of the company's assets (with some exceptions, such as business conducted in the ordinary course of business);
- to the extent that the company breaches the above-described prohibitions, then such acts will be ineffective vis-à-vis creditors.

In addition, if there is an immediate need to protect the assets of the debtor's estate, the insolvency court may – either upon the request of the creditor(s) or at its own discretion – issue a preliminary injunction, whereby the debtor is to some extent restricted in the disposal of its assets. The insolvency court may also appoint a preliminary insolvency trustee who will, most importantly, monitor the assets of the estate and aim to assess the state of the insolvency estate.

(ii) The insolvency court shall decide whether or not the debtor is insolvent: in the event of one or more creditor filing a petition for insolvency without undue delay; and within fifteen days in the event of a debtor's petition (if a moratorium is allowed, within ten days of the termination of the moratorium). The effects of the insolvency court's decision that the debtor is insolvent are as follows:
- if the insolvency court restricted the debtor to a certain extent in the disposal of its assets, such asset disposals can only be effected by the insolvency trustee; and
- the set-off of receivables is only possible where conditions for such set-off had been met prior to the decision on insolvency and further requirements stipulated in the Insolvency Act are met.

Even if the above-mentioned conditions are met, the set-off of receivables is not possible, if:
- a moratorium is approved by the court either before the formal insolvency proceedings against the debtor are started or during such proceedings;
- a proposal for reorganisation is submitted – until the reorganisation plan is either approved and becomes effective or is dismissed; or
- such set-off is prohibited by the court.

The main purpose of this restriction is to give an insolvent debtor a chance to successfully negotiate and complete a reorganisation plan.

(iii) The most serious effects are connected to the declaration of bankruptcy:
- the right to dispose of the debtor's estate pass to the insolvency trustee;
- the powers to exercise rights and to fulfil duties pertaining legally to the entity that is bankrupt pass to the insolvency trustee upon the declaration of bankruptcy if they relate to the disposal of assets belonging to the estate;
- the debtor's debts that are not yet due, provided that these are to be satisfied from the debtor's estate, are regarded as having become payable; and

- the Insolvency Act deals with rules under which the insolvency trustee is entitled to cancel a leasing contract, sub-leasing contract or a rental contract concluded by the bankrupt party; it also stipulates that performance cannot be claimed with respect to fixed-term contracts where the debtor's performance is due after bankruptcy was declared; and
- the Insolvency Act sets out rules under which the insolvency trustee can deal with the performance of bilateral contracts which have not yet been fully performed.

The Insolvency Act Also Sets Out Rules under Which Certain Acts Undertaken by the Debtor Will Become Ineffective

[117] No legal act undertaken by the debtor is ineffective; the ineffectiveness must be claimed by the insolvency trustee at the insolvency court. A petition for ineffectiveness may be filed within one year of the decision on insolvency. In accordance with the Insolvency Act, the debtor's legal acts may be proclaimed ineffective if they constitute:

- 'undervalues', i.e., acts without reasonable consideration;
- 'preferences', i.e., acts in preference of a certain creditor; or
- 'fraudulent transfers', i.e., acts intentionally preventing a creditor from being satisfied.

[118] There are time limits (one to five years prior to the commencement of the insolvency proceedings) within which such legal acts must have taken place. The applicable time limits vary (depending on which of the above reasons apply and depending on whether the entity benefiting from such act is an affiliated entity).

The Insolvency Trustee

[119] The main responsibilities in bankruptcy proceedings are those of the court-appointed insolvency trustee. The right to dispose of the debtor's property is transferred to (i) the preliminary insolvency trustee – if appointed, and to the extent specified in the appointment any time after the commencement of the insolvency proceedings and (ii) the insolvency trustee, after the declaration of bankruptcy up to termination of the insolvency proceedings. The key decisions of the insolvency trustee need to be approved by the court. The insolvency trustee is also controlled by and is obliged to cooperate with the creditors' committee. In the subsequent stages of the insolvency proceedings, the committee or the debtor may ask the court to revoke the insolvency trustee for misconduct or failure to act with due care.

Creditors Committee

[120] A three- to seven-member committee (or the creditors' representative in the event of a low number of creditors – below fifty) is elected by the creditors under the rule 'one crown (CZK) – one vote'. The Insolvency Act provides that all types of creditors should be represented in the committee and the unsecured creditors should be represented by at least the same number of representatives as secured creditors. The committee and its members are given by law extensive responsibilities, including the right to examine the debtor's financial accounts and the debtor's documents to the same extent as the insolvency trustee and the right to present proposals on various steps in the course of the debtor's insolvency.

Conflict of Interest

[121] As a general rule, a creditor who belongs to the same concern (a group of companies with united management) as the debtor or a creditor who is closely related to a debtor, cannot vote at the creditor's meeting. A court may grant an exceptional right to a creditor to vote in these circumstances under the conditions set out by the Insolvency Act.

Assets Realisation

[122] The responsibility of the insolvency trustee is to realise the assets of the company and to ensure the collection of the debts for the creditors. Although the insolvency trustee can continue to operate the company and sell the business as an ongoing concern, this option has not been commonly used in the Czech Republic. The assets can be sold in an involuntary public auction, through a court-managed enforcement procedure or an outside public auction (the consent of the insolvency court and the committee is required). The total proceeds from bankruptcy are generally very low – the unsecured creditors receive on average less than 5% on their receivables.

Moratorium

[123] A debtor (whether an individual or a legal entity) who carries out business activities for profit can request that the court grant it a moratorium. This is a maximum period of three months, in which the debtor can try to overcome its difficulties on its own. Such request for a moratorium can be served to the court either before or after the application for insolvency has been filed (by the debtor itself or by a creditor) with the court.

[124] During this moratorium period, if it is granted, the debtor cannot be declared insolvent. No trustee is appointed to oversee the debtor's dealings unless the debtors or a qualified number of creditors request the appointment of a preliminary trustee.

[125] Creditors' claims arising within the thirty days prior to the commencement of the moratorium or in the course of the moratorium which relate directly to the operation of the debtor's business can be paid by the debtor as and when such claims become due, even prior to the satisfaction of claims due at an earlier time. Further, contracts for utilities or raw materials that have been in place for at least three months at the time of commencement of the moratorium cannot be terminated or repudiated by a party other than the debtor due to the debtor's failure to pay for deliveries. This ensures the delivery of further supplies, thus giving the debtor a fair chance of overcoming the threatened insolvency.

Insolvency Register

[126] The insolvency register is a public register which contains information and documents relating to entities in respect of which insolvency proceedings have been commenced on or after 1 January 2008.

[127] The insolvency register is accessible online at the website of the Ministry of Justice. The insolvency register substantially increases third-party access to information about insolvency proceedings.

[128] The legal effects associated with the opening of insolvency proceedings commence once a notice that insolvency proceedings have been opened has been published in the insolvency register.

The notice that insolvency proceedings have been opened must be published in the insolvency register by the insolvency court within two hours of receipt of an insolvency petition (the date, hour, and minute of publication are recorded), if such petition was received by a court during its business hours; otherwise within two hours of commencement of court business hours.

[129] The insolvency court may delay the publishing of the notice by up to seven days if at the time of receiving the insolvency petition it has reasonable doubts whether the insolvency of the debtor has been proven by the insolvency petition. If the insolvency petition is rejected by the court during this time period for being manifestly unsubstantiated, the court may fine the petitioner up to CZK500 000 (approx. EUR19 000).

Main Practical Problems

Length of the Proceedings

[130] The length of insolvency proceedings under the Insolvency Act has shortened. The Insolvency Act stipulates specific deadlines by which certain steps must be taken. This was not the case under the previous legislation, and bankruptcy cases were commonly open for two to three years.

Secured Creditors

[131] The secured creditor is entitled to satisfy its claim from the sale of the assets over which it has obtained security, after the deduction of the maintenance costs (up to 4% of the proceeds), enforcement costs (up to 5% of the proceeds) and the remuneration of the insolvency trustee (up to 2% of the proceeds). To the extent that the amount of the secured creditor's claim exceeds the value of the security (as determined by an expert valuation), the secured creditor's claim is considered unsecured. Unsecured claims are satisfied pro rata from the remaining assets in the company's estate once all priority claims have been satisfied (insolvency estate claims – i.e., claims against the estate and claims ranking pari passu with the claims against the estate). Subject to several exceptions, there may be sanctions imposed by a court for (i) filing a petition where there is a significant difference (over 50%) between the value of the claim stated in the insolvency petition and the value of the claim assessed in the course of the review hearing and (ii) filing a claim as secured where the creditor is entitled to less than 50% of the value of the claim or when the security has a lower priority (rank) than that claimed by the secured creditor in the petition.

Collateral Provided by Third Parties

[132] The insolvency trustee may not realise the collateral provided by a third party to secure a debtor's liabilities as it is not part of the debtor's estate. The creditors may seek the satisfaction of those of their claims that are secured with collateral owned by third parties outside the insolvency proceedings and participate in the insolvency proceedings against the debtor as unsecured creditors.

Hardening Period

[133] There is no hardening period under the Insolvency Act. The insolvency trustee may in certain cases file a claim for the ineffectiveness of the security, as described in paragraph above.

Distribution of Assets: Priority Claims and Ranking

[134] The Insolvency Act divides creditors primarily into two groups: those holding secured claims and those holding unsecured claims:

(i) A secured creditor has the right to realise a secured asset owned by the debtor. Secured creditors may be satisfied ahead of any claims of other creditors and can instruct the insolvency trustee on the manner of monetisation of the asset(s).

(ii) In addition to secured creditors, there is also another type of claim that is treated specially and has priority over the claims of the unsecured creditors. These so-called claims against the bankruptcy estate (in Czech: '*pohledávky za majetkovou podstatou*') and 'claims that rank pari passu with the claims against the bankruptcy estate' (in Czech: '*pohledávky postavené na roveň pohledávkám za majetkovou podstatou*') will be satisfied before the satisfaction of the claims of any of the unsecured creditors.

These claims, if they were created after the insolvency proceedings were initiated, include, *inter alia*:

(i) (a) The reimbursement of expenses incurred by entities involved in the insolvency proceedings (such as the insolvency trustee, but not the creditors) during the insolvency proceedings; (b) the remuneration of the (preliminary) insolvency trustee, the liquidation trustee and the members of the creditors committee; (c) a refund of the deposit for covering the costs of the insolvency proceedings (if paid by an entity other than the debtor); and the following claims (provided that they were created after the decision on insolvency).

(ii) (a) The reimbursement of the costs borne by third parties that cooperated with the insolvency trustee; (b) the reimbursement of the costs and the remuneration of the expert in relation to the evaluation of the estate; (c) taxes, fees, customs duties, social insurance, contributions to the state employment fund and public health insurance payments.

(iii) Following the satisfaction of the claims of the secured creditors, claims against the bankruptcy estate and claims that rank pari passu with the claims against the bankruptcy estate, the insolvency trustee will prepare a schedule of the satisfaction of all other general unsecured and subordinated claims. Subordinated claims are claims subordinated by operation of law (such as claims of shareholders arising from their participation in an insolvent company) or claims subordinated due to a contractual subordination. Subordinated claims may be satisfied only after all other claims enforced in the insolvency proceedings have been satisfied.

(iv) Any interest, default interest and default payment fees which accrued after the court's decision on insolvency and which became due after the court's decision on insolvency are among claims that are excluded by law from satisfaction in the insolvency proceedings.

Reorganisation

[135] Reorganisation may be used as a method of resolving insolvency only subject to the following conditions:

(a) the debtor is an entrepreneur and the reorganisation pertains to its business;
(b) the debtor (a legal entity) is not in the process of winding up and is not a securities trader or an entity authorised to trade on the commodity exchange; and
(c) the debtor's total turnover in the last accounting period preceding the insolvency petition reached a minimum of CZK50 000 000 (approx. EUR1 850 000) or the debtor employs more than fifty employees whose employment with the debtor constitutes their main employment;
(d) even if the above conditions are not met, reorganisation can be used as a method of resolving insolvency if approved by the majority of creditors (calculated on the basis of the size of their claims).

[136] Any entity filing an insolvency petition shall state in its insolvency petition which method of resolving the insolvency it deems most appropriate. Further, the debtor or any of its creditors may propose reorganisation as a method of resolving the insolvency no later than ten days before the meeting of creditors scheduled to take place after the decision on insolvency.

[137] If the conditions for reorganisation are not met, the insolvency court rules that the insolvency of the debtor will be resolved by bankruptcy. Conversely, if the reorganisation is also available as a method of resolving insolvency, the meeting of creditors scheduled to take place after the issuance of the decision of insolvency can decide on which method of insolvency will be used. In such case, the insolvency official must present to the meeting of creditors a report summarising its activities since the date of the decision on insolvency and containing its view on the proposed method of insolvency.

[138] A resolution of the meeting of creditors on the method of resolving insolvency requires the consent of a majority of both the secured and unsecured creditors present at the meeting of creditors (calculated on the basis of the size of their claims) or by 90% of all creditors present at the meeting of creditors (calculated on the basis of the size of their claims). If the resolution on the method of resolving insolvency is so adopted, the insolvency court will respect the method of resolving the insolvency preferred by the creditors and will issue its own decision on resolving the insolvency in accordance with the resolution of the meeting of creditors. The insolvency court shall issue a decision on the method of resolving the insolvency within three months of the date of the decision on insolvency.

[139] Reorganisation is carried out in line with a reorganisation plan, which must be approved by the creditors and the insolvency court. The debtor retains its right to dispose of and act on behalf of its business, and its dealings are supervised by the trustee and the creditors. Reorganisation may consist of a variety of measures, including, but not limited to, the restructuring of debts by means of a partial discharge or by postponing maturity dates, the sale of assets, a merger with other entities, issuing shares or other securities or arranging for debt financing.

[140] If the debtor does not comply with the reorganisation plan, which is being overseen by the creditors and the insolvency trustee, then the reorganisation will end in bankruptcy.

CHOICE OF LAW

Choice of Law

[141] The choice of a foreign law to govern an agreement entered into by a Czech party will be valid under the conditions stipulated by Regulation (EC) No. 593/2008 of the European Parliament and of the Council of 17 June 2008 on the Law Applicable to Contractual Obligations (Rome I).

[142] It is strongly recommended that agreements relating to assets registered in public registers (real estate, ownership interest in a limited liability company) or rights to be entered into public registers or a notarial register (e.g., negative pledge, pledge of receivables) be governed by Czech law.

Jurisdiction

[143] Judgments obtained in other member countries of the European Union are enforceable in the Czech Republic in line with the Regulation No. 1215/2012 of the European Parliament and of the Council of 12 December 2012 on jurisdiction and the recognition and enforcement of judgments in civil and commercial matters and Private International Law Act.

[144] The Hague Convention on Choice of Court Agreements is effective in the Czech Republic from 1 October 2015. It has been so far signed and ratified by Denmark, EU, Mexico, Montenegro, Singapore, and the United Kingdom. Ratification is pending in China, Ukraine and the United States of America (USA).

[145] Under general statutory regulations, a decision of a foreign court shall not be recognised and enforced in the Czech Republic, for example, if:

(a) the matter is one that is within the exclusive jurisdiction of the Czech courts, pursuant to its laws, or if the proceedings could not be conducted before any court or authority of the foreign country if the rules on the jurisdiction of Czech courts were used to determine whether such foreign court had jurisdiction; or
(b) a final decision on the same matter has previously been reached by a court of authority in the Czech Republic or a final decision of an authority or court of a third state in respect of the same matter has previously been recognised in the Czech Republic; or
(c) the party against whom the enforcement of such judgment is sought has been deprived of the opportunity to participate in the foreign proceedings, especially if the summons or notice of the commencement of the foreign proceedings was not personally served on the defendant or his authorised agent; or
(d) recognition of the foreign judgment would be contrary to the public policy (in Czech: '*veřejný pořádek*') of the Czech Republic; or
(e) reciprocal enforcement of judgments of courts of the Czech Republic is not afforded by the foreign country concerned (however, reciprocity is not required if the judgment is not against a citizen or a legal entity resident in the Czech Republic).

Arbitration

[146] An arbitral award or decision of an arbitral tribunal will be recognised and enforced in the Czech Republic in accordance with, and subject to, the New York Convention on Recognition and Enforcement of Foreign Arbitral Awards made at New York on 10 June 1958 and Private International Law Act.

MOST COMMON ACQUISITION TRANSACTIONS

Types of Transactions

[147] The most commonly used acquisition transactions are:

(a) the acquisition of shares in a joint-stock company;
(b) the acquisition of an ownership interest in a limited liability company;
(c) the acquisition of company's assets; and
(d) the acquisition of company's business or a part thereof.

General Information

[148] The parties are free to determine the rights and obligations of the acquisition agreement as they see fit, as long as the mandatory provisions of Czech law are fulfilled. In addition, various procedural requirements apply to each of these acquisition methods. The number and type of procedural requirements that must be fulfilled in order to carry out the selected acquisition method should also be considered with respect to timing and indirect acquisition costs in particular. From the procedural point of view, the acquisition of shares in a joint-stock company or an ownership interest in a limited liability company or the acquisition of assets are the least complicated, while the acquisition of an enterprise (or a part thereof) or a lease of an enterprise require more procedural steps be taken. The lease of an enterprise is the least common type of acquisition transactions.

[149] During negotiations, it is quite common for the parties to execute a letter of intent or a memorandum of understanding setting out certain terms of the transaction. Under certain circumstances, a party could be liable for damages, if it unjustifiably terminated the negotiations.

Transfer of Liabilities

[150] The new body of private law contains several provisions that qualify the rules relating to asset deals valid under the legal regulation effective until 31 December 2013 – i.e., that liabilities do not transfer along with individual assets, unless a particular liability is transferred by operation of law (e.g., mortgage, pledge, easement, lease contracts).

[151] The new Civil Code stipulates that:

– A person who acquires an ownership right also acquires the rights and obligations connected to the asset.

- A person who acquires an ownership right to an asset registered in a public register encumbered with a pledge or mortgage or other surety is also deemed to have assumed the debt secured by such encumbrance.
- A person who assumes all or a part of another person's assets becomes a joint and several debtor together with the transferor of the debts which are related to the assumed assets and of which the acquirer knew or must have known when entering into the agreement. The maximum amount the acquirer may be required to pay is limited to the value of assets which he acquired. This limit does not apply when the acquisition is carried out between related parties, unless the acquirer proves that he was not aware nor was he required to be aware of the debt.

[152] The above-described rules on transfer of liabilities apply not only to acquisition of individual assets (buildings, land, machinery) but also to acquisition of shares.

Representations and Warranties

[153] The concept of representations and warranties and the consequences of their breach are not explicitly regulated under Czech law. Notwithstanding this fact, representations and warranties have become a standard contractual clause in agreements governed by Czech law. The validity of such clauses has been confirmed by several decisions of the Czech Supreme Court.

[154] Parties to a Czech-law governed agreement that want to rely on representations and warranties (i) include an explicit statement in the agreement that the promising party acknowledges and accepts the other party's reliance on the representations and warranties relating to the subject matter of the agreement, and (ii) specify in the agreement the consequences of a representation and/or warranty turning out to be untrue, inaccurate and/or misleading (to put the counterparty in the same position as if the breach did not occur, e.g., by a discount from the purchase price, a right to withdraw from the agreement, damages, payment of costs, contractual penalty).

Acquisition of Shares in a Joint-Stock Company

Transfer of Shares

[155] The method of transferring a title to the shares depends on the type of share that is being transferred.

[156] The title to all types of shares is transferred by virtue of a share purchase agreement ('*SPA*').

[157] In the case of a transfer of registered certificated shares, the endorsement and delivery of the shares to the purchaser is also required to complete the transfer.

The endorsement must identify the purchaser and contain the signature of the seller.

[158] In the case of a transfer of book-entered shares, the registration of the security on the owner's account in the Central Securities Depository is needed, in addition to the signing of an SPA.

[159] The parties can agree in writing on the date of the title transfer, which may be any date following the execution of the SPA and may be conditional on fulfilment of various conditions precedent to the transfer. However, for the transfer to be effective on the agreed day, the certificated shares must be also handed over to the buyer on that day.

[160] The articles of association of a joint-stock company may restrict, but not exclude, the transferability of registered shares.

[161] A transfer of registered certificated shares is effective in relation to a joint-stock company only when the transfer is evidenced and the shares are presented to the joint-stock company. A joint-stock company must maintain a register of shareholders unless it issues book-entered shares and the articles of association stipulate that the register at the Central Securities Depository replaces the joint-stock company's shareholders' register.

[162] A buyer of shares acting in good faith acquires good title to the shares even if the seller did not originally have good title. Under specific circumstances, invalidly issued shares can be acquired in good faith. However, this does not apply to shares which do not contain all elements required by Czech law and which consequently are invalid. The acquisition of such invalid shares is invalid even if such shares were acquired in good faith. Given that shortcomings in producing valid shares occur quite often, an investor should always conduct a proper check of any shares that it plans to purchase.

[163] The transfer of certificated shares does not require an entry in the Commercial Register or other similar registry. However, if a joint-stock company has a sole shareholder, that shareholder must be registered in the Commercial Register. This makes the joint-stock company a more suitable corporate form if it is anticipated that the shares will change hands frequently. Furthermore, the joint-stock company is the only form of investment vehicle in the Czech Republic whose shares may be listed on a stock exchange and offered for sale to the general public.

Consequences of the Acquisition of Shares

[164] The acquisition of shares has, in particular, the following consequences:

(a) The buyer acquires a shareholding in the company with all its existing assets and liabilities, including current and contingent tax and environmental liabilities. This also applies to any liabilities not disclosed in the accounts or during the due diligence process.
(b) The buyer of shares listed for trading on stock exchanges will have various reporting duties regarding the number of shares held by the buyer and also

by entities acting in concert with the buyer. Furthermore, it may, upon exceeding certain thresholds, be obliged to carry out a mandatory buy-out.

(c) The buyer acquires a shareholding in the company with all public law licences and permits issued to it. If the company has any such licences or permits, the acquisition may be subject to the notification of or the approval of the relevant authorities.

(d) The buyer becomes liable to pay up any outstanding capital contribution related to the shares. However, the seller is, by operation of law, a guarantor of the buyer's obligation to pay up the shares. Unpaid shares may be represented by an interim share certificate, which is registered in the name of the shareholder to whom the certificate was first issued and which is transferable by endorsement. The buyer, however, is not liable for any other liabilities of the joint-stock company.

(e) Unlike some transactions involving the transfer of assets, no approval by the boards or the general meeting of the target joint-stock company is required for the sale of shares except that the articles of association may require the approval of the general meeting in relation to registered shares only. Approval of a general meeting would be required if the sale / purchase of shares constituted the disposal / acquisition of a significant part of an enterprise of the seller / buyer.

(f) Generally, either (i) the seller's (or the buyer's) corporate documents or (ii) the law governing their incorporation may require additional consents for an acquisition.

Issues to Be Considered in Share Deals

[165]

(a) The possible use of the assets of the acquired joint-stock company as security for financing the acquisition is limited if the transaction is regarded as constituting the provision of 'financial assistance' by the target company.

(b) The cash flow generated by the assets of the target joint-stock company, as well as any proceeds from the sale of the target joint-stock company's assets, accrue to the target joint-stock company itself; the use of such cash flow for the purposes of financing the acquisition of such target joint-stock company by the buyer may also lead to the transaction being seen as the provision of financial assistance by the target company.

(c) Although contracts binding on the target joint-stock company generally remain in force, the potential buyer should become aware of any possible termination clauses in such contracts entitling the counterparty to terminate the contract in the event of any change of control. Such termination clauses are, for example, common in financing arrangements.

(d) A buyer of less than 100% of the shares in a joint-stock company should verify: (i) the level of the various majority requirements for adopting decisions of the target joint-stock company's general meeting, so that it can plan the purchase of the number shares required to effectively control the joint-stock company, and (ii) the rights of the remaining minority shareholders. Some of these requirements are stipulated directly by the Business Corporations Act and some may be stipulated in the articles of association.

(e) An SPA may also be governed by laws other than Czech law as long as the mandatory provisions regarding the manner of transfer of the title to the shares are observed.
(f) A foreign governing law may be selected for shareholders' agreements relating to a Czech company.

Squeeze-Out with Transfer of Shares to the Majority Shareholder

[166] The Business Corporations Act allows a shareholder who has shares representing at least 90% of the registered capital and 90% of the voting rights in a joint-stock company the right to enforce the transfer of the shares of the remaining shareholders to it for fair compensation. The company survives the squeeze-out and the majority shareholder acquires a 100% shareholding in the company. Unlike in other jurisdictions where it is only possible to use this technique to squeeze out shareholders in listed companies, in the Czech Republic, it is possible to use this type of squeeze-out in unlisted companies as well.

[167] The squeeze-out procedure involves, in particular, the following steps:

(a) approval of the squeeze-out by the general meeting of the company;
(b) determination of the compensation paid to minority shareholders on the basis of an expert opinion;
(c) an expert opinion is not required in the case of securities traded on the Regulated Market. In this case, the majority shareholder must justify the price in writing and obtain the prior approval of the Czech National Bank;
(d) preparation of certain documents by the majority shareholder and their delivery to the company;
(e) publication of certain information relating to the squeeze-out in the same manner as notification of the convocation of the general meeting of the company;
(f) deposition of certain documents at the registered seat of the company; and
(g) registration of the squeeze-out in the Commercial Register;
(h) The ownership right to the shares is transferred to the majority shareholder by operation of law after the lapse of a one-month period commencing on the day following the day of the publication of a notice in the Commercial Bulletin that the resolution of the general meeting of the company approving the squeeze-out has been registered in the Commercial Register.

Acquisition of an Ownership Interest in a Limited Liability Company

[168] As an ownership interest in a limited liability company is most often not represented by certificated securities, slightly different rules apply to its transfer in comparison with shares in a joint-stock company.

[169] Unless the parties stipulate otherwise, an ownership interest in a limited liability company is transferred upon the relevant SPA becoming effective. The SPA must be in writing, and the signatures of both parties must be notarised. If signed outside the Czech Republic (including in the EU), an apostille or superlegalisation may be required.

[170] An ownership interest may also be incorporated into a security called a 'common certificate'. As this option has existed only since 1 January 2014, not many companies have taken advantage of it yet.

[171] In this case, an ownership interest is transferred by transferring the common certificate. A common certificate can be transferred by means of an oral/written SPA, an endorsement and the hand-over of the common certificate. The transfer is subsequently registered in the Commercial Register.

[172] After the duly executed and effective SPA has been delivered to the company (or in the case of a transfer of a common certificate, after a change of the member of the company has been notified to the company and a common certificate has been presented to the company), an executive director is required to arrange for the registration of the change in the Commercial Register.

[173] From 1 January 2014, it is no longer required to file one counterpart of the SPA in the public collection of documents maintained by the Commercial Register.

[174] When determining the requirements for the transfer of an ownership interest, the provisions of the limited liability company's memorandum of association are decisive.

[175] The transfer of an ownership interest to another shareholder does not require the approval of the limited liability company's general meeting, unless the need for such approval is explicitly stipulated under the memorandum of association. The memorandum of association may contain additional restrictions on transfer of an ownership interest.

[176] The transfer of an ownership interest to a non-shareholder requires the approval of the general meeting, unless the memorandum of association stipulates otherwise.

[177] If the company has a sole shareholder, the ownership interest is transferable without restrictions.

[178] Czech law no longer contains a restriction on the 'chaining' of limited liability companies. This means that a limited liability company with a sole shareholder may be the sole founder of or the sole shareholder in another limited liability company.

[179] Czech law contained the chaining restriction until 31 December 2013. According to the prevailing view of leading legal practitioners, this restriction also applied to foreign entities. Consequently, a foreign entity with a sole shareholder could not be the sole founder of or the sole shareholder in a Czech limited liability company.

[180] Therefore, the acquisition transaction had to be structured in such a manner that (i) there was more than one shareholder in the limited liability company after the transfer, or (ii) the new sole shareholder of the limited liability company was not a limited liability company with a sole shareholder.

[181] Transfers contrary to this prohibition were invalid and any buyer that breached the chaining prohibition could not become a member of a Czech limited liability company.

[182] As the removal of the chaining prohibition has not remedied invalid transfers that were undertaken before 1 January 2014, it is still important to conduct a proper legal due diligence of the title to the ownership interest.

Acquisition of Assets

General

[183] In an asset purchase transaction, the assets (tangible and/or intangible), are transferred individually and each must be precisely specified in the transaction documentation.

Specification of Assets and Liabilities

[184] The exact specification of all the assets (both tangible and intangible) to be transferred is vital for the enforceability of the transfer agreement. Where large numbers of assets are to be transferred, the individual assets are usually listed in an annex to the transfer agreement. It is not usually sufficient to refer to the balance sheet of a company for identification of assets, as the balance sheet may also include assets that the company does not own, or it may not show all the company's assets. In addition, there may be an interim period between the signing of the agreement and completion and, therefore, it may be necessary to stipulate that the list of assets in the annex is subject to change in the normal course of business. A provision for the disclosure of the completion accounts would be the normal method of assessing and identifying the state of the assets upon completion.

Acquisition of an Enterprise or a Part Thereof

[185] Another form of capital transfer under Czech law is the sale of an enterprise. An enterprise is deemed to be constituted by the aggregate of debts and assets which an entrepreneur created and which serve the operation of an enterprise. It is a collective thing (*hromadná věc*). It is not a legal person. Given that an enterprise comprises both assets and liabilities it can also have a negative value.

[186] The effect of a contract for the sale of an enterprise is that all rights and obligations pertaining to the enterprise pass to the buyer. It is possible to sell an enterprise, or a part thereof. Czech law also allows for the lease of an enterprise or a part thereof.

[187] The new Civil Code does not clearly stipulate a moment at which a transfer of an enterprise takes effect. The relevant provisions of the legal regulations are in contradiction – a transfer of enterprise becomes effective either when the information about the transfer is published in the Commercial Gazette or when the transfer agreement is published in the online Collection of Documents maintained by the Commercial Register. Due to a relatively short life of the new Civil Code, this issue has not been interpreted by the courts yet and thus no binding interpretation exists. The prevailing interpretation seems to be that the transfer is effective when the transfer agreement is published in the Collection of Documents maintained by the Commercial Register. Such publication is completed by a court clerk by (i) filing the transfer agreement in the Collection of Documents; (ii) uploading the transfer agreement to the online version of the Collection of Documents; and (iii) stating the date of such publication. A judge of a Czech Supreme Court has expressed a view in an academic article that parties can set the transfer date in the transfer agreement.

[188] Only an agreement (without registration of the transfer in the Commercial Gazette or the Collection of deeds) is required for a transfer of an enterprise to become effective if the buyer is not registered in the Commercial Register.

[189] The buyer of an enterprise acquires by operation of law:

(a) all rights and liabilities relating to the enterprise being sold. Only liabilities of which the buyer was aware of or must have reasonably assumed that existed are passed to the buyer;
(b) all intellectual property rights related to the enterprise, except for rights whose transfer would conflict with any agreement between the parties on the provision of a particular intellectual property right or the nature of such right;
(c) all rights and obligations of the seller arising from labour contracts with the employees of the enterprise.

[190] Certain elements attributable to the seller rather than to the enterprise do not pass to the purchaser. The items not transferred include the majority of public law licences, unless the relevant laws provide otherwise, and public liabilities, such as tax liabilities.

[191] The parties are free to agree on the purchase price. If not determined by the parties, the purchase price is determined under the Business Corporations Act on the basis of the assets and liabilities in the accounting records for the enterprise as at the day that the sale contract was signed and on the basis of other values stipulated in the contract. If the date of effectiveness is later than the date of signing, the price is adjusted based on any changes in business assets that have occurred.

Transfer Process: Approvals and Registrations

[192] The transfer must be approved by the general meetings of the seller and the buyer. In the case of a joint-stock company, the general meeting resolution must be in the form of a notarial deed. In the case of a limited liability company, the general meeting resolution does not have to be in the form of a notarial deed.

Protection of Creditors

[193] If a creditor does not consent to the assumption of debt by the buyer, the seller guarantees the settlement of the debt.

[194] The Seller is obliged to inform its creditors and debtors of the sale of the enterprise and of the identity of the buyer.

[195] If a creditor's position deteriorates due to the sale of an enterprise, the creditor who disagreed with the sale may challenge the transfer of its receivable from the seller to the buyer in court.

[196] This right of the creditor expires one month from the day on which the creditor learned of the sale, but at the latest years from effectiveness of a transfer agreement.

Part of an Enterprise

[197] The above rules also apply to the sale of part of an enterprise.

SPECIFIC RULES ON PUBLIC TAKEOVERS

General

[198] Takeover offers have not been a common technique for acquiring control over joint-stock companies in the Czech Republic. Most often, controlling stakes in joint-stock companies are transferred in privately negotiated deals or in tenders organised by the government in the process of the privatisation of state-owned property.

Barriers to Takeovers

Corporate Governance

[199] The crucial legal question for the buyer to address is what level of shareholding is necessary to acquire an effective control of the target joint-stock company.

[200] The articles of association of a joint-stock company are the main instrument determining the rights of a majority shareholder. A general meeting has a quorum if shareholders whose shares represent at least 30% of the registered capital are present, unless the articles of association prescribe a higher quorum. A simple majority vote of shareholders present is required to adopt decisions at the general meeting, unless the Business Corporations Act or the articles of association state a higher majority. Majority requirements are arguably the most important defensive tactic employed to prevent hostile takeovers. A two-thirds majority is required to change the articles of association or to increase or decrease the registered capital. A three-quarters majority is required to change the type or form of shares, change the rights of a type of shares, restrict the transferability of registered shares, de-list shares, restrict or cancel the pre-emptive rights of shareholders, or increase the registered capital by non-monetary contributions.

[201] Members of the board of directors and supervisory board are typically elected by the general meeting by a simple majority vote. The articles of association may provide for a higher quorum or stipulate that members of the board of directors are elected by the supervisory board.

Restricted Registered Shares

[202] The articles of association may restrict, but not completely prohibit, the transfer of registered shares. If the conditions for a share transfer are not met, the share transfer agreement is not valid unless the acquirer was in good faith. If one of the conditions for transfer is the consent of a corporate body of the target joint-stock company, the share transfer agreement will not become effective until such consent is given, and the parties are entitled to terminate the agreement if it does not become effective within six months of signing. *See also* the breakthrough rule in paragraphs **[26]–[32]** above.

Financial Aspects

[203] A joint-stock company is prohibited from providing financial assistance for the purpose of financing the acquisition of its shares (*see* details in paragraphs [89] and [90]). The joint-stock company may not repay shareholder contributions. Furthermore, all payments to shareholders are prohibited, with the exception of dividends from net profits approved by the general meeting.

Defence Tactics and Duties of the Board of Directors

[204] Many defence tactics used in the course of takeover battles, in particular, those used in the United States or the United Kingdom, may not be legal or workable in the Czech Republic.

[205] From the time the members of the board of directors or the supervisory board of the target company receive reasonably reliable information that a takeover offer will be made, they:

(i) must not pass measures that could prevent the addressees of the takeover offer from knowing the relevant facts and deciding freely on the takeover offer; and

(ii) must refrain from any acts that could frustrate the offer until the results of the offer are published, unless:
  (a) such particular acts are approved by the general meeting of the target company during the time allowed for acceptance of the offer;
  (b) the target company is fulfilling the obligations imposed by legal regulations; or
  (c) the act is made in the course of the target's company standard business operations.

[206] Members of the board of directors or the supervisory board of the target company may seek, even without the general meeting's approval, a competing takeover offer.

[207] A competing takeover offer may also be made by the members of the board of directors or the supervisory board themselves.

[208] Within five business days of delivery of the offer document to the members of the board of directors and the supervisory board of the target company, such members are obliged to prepare a joint statement regarding the takeover offer, stating, in particular, whether the offer follows the interests of the target company, the addressees of the offer and the employees and creditors of the target company.

[209] The statement must be delivered to the offeror and the CNB no later than two business days after it has been prepared.

OTHER RELEVANT LAWS, ANTI-BRIBERY

Anti-bribery Laws

[210] Under Czech law, a bribe means any unjustified advantage of direct asset enrichment or other benefits that the bribed person is to receive or with their consent give to another person and to which they are otherwise not entitled *('Bribe')*. Crimes of corruption might also be committed by a company (*see* below in paragraphs [214] and [215]). Three different crimes of corruption are recognised:

(i) **Passive bribery** – a person commits the crime of passive bribery if he requests or accepts, either by themselves or through another person, a Bribe (or the promise of a Bribe), for themselves or for another person, in connection with (a) the procurement of goods of general interest or (b) an enterprise. The maximum sentence for passive bribery is twelve years of imprisonment. The crime of passive bribery becomes statute-barred after fifteen years.

(ii) **Active bribery** – a person commits the crime active bribery if he provides, offers or promises a Bribe to another person in relation to (a) the procurement of goods of general interest or (b) a business. The maximum sentence for active bribery is six years' imprisonment. The crime of active bribery becomes statute-barred after ten years.

(iii) **Indirect bribery** – a person also commits the crime of indirect bribery if he requests or accepts a Bribe in return for using his/her influence or the influence of a third party to affect the performance of the office of an official person. A person who provides, promises or offers a Bribe for the purpose mentioned in the previous sentence also commits indirect bribery. The maximum sentence for indirect bribery is three years' imprisonment. The crime of indirect bribery becomes statute-barred after five years.

[211] It follows from the above that bribery is considered to be a crime regardless of whether the Bribe was given/offered to a public official or whether it has been given/offered in a business transaction between two private individuals/companies. However, the most commonly prosecuted cases still relate to the bribery of public officials.

[212] Recently, it has seemed that the police and state prosecutors are increasing their efforts to fight corruption. While the amount of commenced criminal prosecutions relating to corruption crimes actually fell in the last years, many cases of bribery often relate to public procurement, and the prosecution of crimes related to public procurement has been rising. Furthermore, several high-profile criminal prosecutions relating to bribery (involving several top politicians) have been initiated.

[213] In addition, the 'long reach' of the United States' Foreign Corrupt Practices Act(FCPA) or the United Kingdom (UK) Bribery Act has an effect on the M&A transactions, as foreign investors often undertake anti-bribery due diligence before acquiring a Czech target (especially if the target operates in a risky sector, such as the construction industry).

Act on the Criminal Liability of Legal Entities

General Information

[214] On 1 January 2012, the Czech Republic joined the increasing number of countries that criminally prosecute legal entities.

[215] The new concept of the criminal liability of legal entities should simplify the prosecution of crimes in cases when it is not possible to prosecute a specific individual but it is obvious that a crime was committed for the benefit of a legal entity. Certain acts committed by individuals can be attributed directly to a legal entity. Such legal entity would then have the possibility to exonerate itself by proving that it had put in place adequate procedures to prevent illegal acts being committed by any of its employees. ACLLE has a significant extra-territorial effect. It is therefore possible that a Czech legal entity which has engaged in corruption abroad or in the Czech Republic and which carries on business activity in (e.g.,) the United Kingdom could be prosecuted under both ACLLE and foreign anti-corruption legislation (e.g., the United States' FCPA or the UK Bribery Act).

Extra-Territorial Effects

[216] The new legislation has extra-territorial effects. The scope of ACLLE is not limited to companies with a registered seat in the Czech Republic but also includes foreign companies who have an enterprise or a branch in the Czech Republic or who carry on their activities or have any property in the Czech Republic. Moreover, crimes committed abroad by a Czech legal entity fall within the scope of ACLLE. Finally, even a crime committed abroad and by a company which does not have its registered seat in the Czech Republic could be prosecuted under ACLLE if it commits a crime for the benefit of a Czech legal entity.

'Attributability' of Acts Committed by Certain Individuals to a Legal Entity

[217] The concept of legal liability is based on the concept of the 'attributability' to a legal entity of acts committed by certain individuals. A legal entity is therefore liable not only for acts committed by the members of its executive body but also for acts committed by other individuals who are authorised to act for or on behalf of the legal entity, individuals who perform managing or controlling activity (or employees or individuals in similar positions while performing work tasks), and even legal entities (e.g., a parent company) that exercise a prevailing influence on the management of such legal entity. For instance, an illegal act committed by a legal or other agent of a legal entity can be attributed to such legal entity.

Necessity to Put in Place Adequate Prevention Procedures (Compliance Rules)

[218] A legal entity can, in certain circumstances, be exculpated from criminal liability. It is liable for a crime only if it has not adopted adequate procedures to prevent the crime or to remove the effects of the crime and even if it did not cause such effects by intention or negligence. In practice, this means that a legal entity must prove that it put in place all procedures necessary to prevent wrongful conduct (e.g., it examined the credibility of its agents and suppliers).

[219] In certain cases, the legal entity can be freed from criminal liability if it manifests genuine remorse and if it voluntarily refrains from further wrongful conduct and mitigates the effects of the crime (or even if it reports the crime in question to the law enforcement authorities). Such exculpation is, however, not possible in the case of corruption crimes.

Succession of Criminal Liability to Legal Successors

[220] The criminal liability of a legal entity passes to all its legal successors. When considering the punishment for each of the successors, the relevant court will consider the extent to which the benefits from crimes passed to such successor.

Sanctions

[221] The penalties and protective measures for crimes committed by legal entities include:

(i) the dissolution of the legal entity;
(ii) the forfeiture of its property;
(iii) a fine;
(iv) the prohibition of certain activities;
(v) a prohibition on taking part in public procurement, concession proceedings or competitive bidding;
(vi) a prohibition on receiving grants or subsidies;
(vii) the publication of the judgment.

[222] The catalogue of crimes which can be attributed to a legal entity is very broad and is not limited to corruption cases, as is the case with other foreign legislation (e.g., the UK Bribery Act, which deals only with corruption).

Enforcement Trends

[223] Even though the ACLLE was adopted only recently, it seems that the police and state prosecutors are often willing to prosecute legal entities. In 2018, a total of 286 legal entities were criminally prosecuted[3]. The crimes for which legal entities were prosecuted included mostly tax evasion, but there were several cases related to corruption, fraud or environmental crimes. Prosecuted legal entities include one of the major Czech construction companies, which is being prosecuted for corruption.

[224] Due to the length of criminal proceedings, there has been only about 443 final judgments so far (completed prosecutions usually related to non-complex cases of tax evasion). However, a 'capital punishment' (i.e., a dissolution) has already been imposed on several companies, mostly for tax evasion.

Money-Laundering Regulations

[225] Under Czech law, money laundering is regulated by Act No. 253/2008, on Certain Measures Against Legalisation of Proceeds from Crime and Financing of Terrorism (the '*AML Act*'), which implements EU Directive No. 2005/60/EC. The

[3] Supreme State Prosecution Office report on activities of the state prosecution (2016).

AML Act stipulates certain obligations for financial institutions but also some other persons/entities dealing with transactions (such as attorneys or notaries when handling escrow payments). For all transactions exceeding EUR1 000, the AML Act stipulates an obligation to identify the client. If the value of the transaction exceeds EUR15 000, a customer due diligence must be performed. The AML Act also stipulates a reporting obligation in respect of suspicious transactions (e.g., unusually large transactions, or transactions without apparent economic or visible lawful purpose).

[226] The Czech law also prohibits (with certain exceptions) cash payments exceeding CZK270 000 (approx. EUR10 000).

[227] The money laundering (or enabling of money laundering) is a crime which can be punishable by up to eight years of imprisonment (or up to five years, if the enablement of the crime arose through negligence). Companies can also be liable for this crime (*see* above in 0).

[228] The enforcement of money-laundering regulations has increased over time, in particular due to the activities of the Financial Analytical Unit of the Ministry of Finance. In 2018, the Financial Analytical Unit seized almost CZK7.5 bn. Furthermore, the Financial Analytical Unit filed 395 criminal complaints in 2018.[4]

THE DUE DILIGENCE PROCESS

General Introduction

[229] Purchasers carry out investigation of the legal, financial, technological and environmental position of a target, and all relevant and related circumstances.

[230] Legal due diligence is generally prepared once the seller has committed to sell the target and the purchaser has decided to acquire the target, often by signing a 'letter of intent', or has submitted a preliminary non-binding offer based on initial information provided by the seller and has, based on such offer, been granted exclusivity for negotiations with the seller for a certain period of time. At this stage, all related and relevant legal relations, the validity of existing agreements and other legal matters must be clarified so that a final decision in respect of the acquisition may be taken.

Specific Issues to Be Reviewed

[231] When acquiring a Czech company whose (or its legal predecessor's) history goes back before 1990, any assets of such company or assets acquired from such

[4] Financial Analytical Unit 2018 annual report.

company, special attention should be paid to reviewing the accuracy of the privatisation process. This requirement applies especially in relation to the ownership of shares in such company, its real estate and intellectual property rights. Due to the hectic nature of the times, the lack of experience and the ambiguity of laws valid at the time, some of the privatisations of state property, especially those in the beginning of the 1990s, were not performed properly. Some of the mistakes that occurred during the privatisation process might still have a material adverse effect on an acquisition carried out now.

Disclosure Restriction

General

[232]

(i) Generally, even the majority shareholder (a seller) is not entitled to order the target company to provide any information to a third party (a purchaser) for the purpose of a due diligence review, unless it is allowed to do so under the Memorandum/Articles of Association of the target company or the target company forms part of a declared concern. Therefore, any due diligence process requires cooperation with the representatives of both the seller and the target company as the representatives of the target company are solely responsible for its business management and are obliged to act in its best interest, i.e., independently from its shareholders, whose interests may differ from those of the company.

(ii) During due diligence, certain documents and items of information are disclosed to the purchaser and/or its professional advisors. In doing so, various legal restrictions must be observed. Thus, an investor will only gain access to certain kinds of information (as defined below) when committing itself to comply with security measures adopted by the target company to avoid the abuse or disclosure of such information by the purchaser or its professional advisors. Such measures are commonly set out in the form of a confidentiality agreement concluded between the target company and the purchaser/its professional advisors and in the form of binding data room rules.

Business Secret

[233]

(i) A business secret includes information that is not commonly available in business circles and that its holder requires to be kept confidential. In the course of due diligence, a reviewer will usually encounter business secrets of the target company as well as business secrets of the entities in contractual (or other) relationships with the target company.

(ii) It is at the sole discretion of the target company whether business secrets shall be disclosed to the purchaser and to decide the terms and conditions for such disclosure. This freedom of disclosure is not absolute as the parties are still bound by the restrictions stipulated by the Competition Act. Disclosure of business secrets during due diligence shall not result in a prohibited information exchange between competitors on either a horizontal or vertical level which could lead to distortion of competition.

(iii) In relation to information classified as a business secret by third parties, unless the third party consented to data disclosure, the target company shall ensure a level of protection corresponding to the scope of protection it owes to the respective third party.

Personal Data Protection

[234]

(i) Personal data means any information relating to an identified or identifiable individual, defined as a 'data subject' (not applicable to data concerning legal entities). The target company is only entitled to disclose personal data upon the consent of the relevant data subject or in cases where an exemption is stipulated by Act No. 110/2019 Coll., as amended, on Processing of Personal Data.

(ii) There is no explicit exemption for the disclosure of personal data within the scope of due diligence. However, it is the prevailing view that such disclosure is allowed provided that the disclosure is essential for the protection of the rights of the target company. Generally, in the event of any disclosure of personal data, adequate protection of the data subject's private and personal life must always be ensured.

Banking Secret

[235]

(i) Under the Banking Act, all information on banking transactions and financial services of banks, including account balances and deposits, shall be the subject of a banking secret. This applies to information concerning both individuals and legal entities.

(ii) Generally, a bank is prohibited from providing information considered a banking secret without its customer's consent unless a specific exemption provided by the Banking Act stipulates otherwise. As there is neither a special regulation nor specific exemption for disclosure of banking secrets in the scope of the due diligence process, measures must be adopted to ensure an adequate level of protection for the disclosed information.

(iii) The due diligence process shall be governed by a confidentiality agreement concluded between the target company and the investor. Any information subject to the banking secrecy rules can only be disclosed to the purchaser's professional and independent advisors. Moreover, the reports prepared by the professional advisors for the purchaser shall contain information in an anonymous or aggregate form only (i.e., without disclosing the identity of the bank's client).

Other Restrictions

[236]

(i) Restrictions similar to those relating to banking secrets apply to information on the insurance policies of both individuals and corporate entities pursuant to the Insurance Act and pension insurance policies under the Pension Funds Act. The Insurance Act provides explicitly for two instances in which an insurance company is entitled to disclose restricted information without its client's consent – firstly, when necessary for disposal of the insurance company's receivables towards its clients, secondly in the case of a contemplated disposal of the insurance policies portfolio. Nevertheless, even these two instances do not relieve the insurance company of the obligation to ensure the protection of the disclosed information in the manner described above.

(ii) A specific confidentiality duty relates to information affecting the legitimate interest of an investment company, investment fund or shareholders and trustees under the Collective Investment Act.

(iii) The Capital Markets Act imposes a general confidentiality duty on certain entities with respect to information that could potentially be important for the assessment of the trends on the capital markets or potentially harm an entity using the services rendered on the capital markets before such information was made public.

(iv) In addition to this general confidentiality duty, the Capital Markets Act also contains a special regime for the protection of 'inside information'.

(v) Inside information is defined under Czech law as information of a precise nature relating, directly or indirectly, to:
   (a) a financial instrument, which is an investment instrument or other instrument, that was admitted to trading on the Regulated Market or for which admission to trading on the Regulated Market has been sought;
   (b) a derivative financial instrument, which is an instrument that has not been admitted to trading on the Regulated Market and whose value derives from the value of a financial instrument;
   (c) the issuer of a financial instrument; or
   (d) any other fact with significant effect on the quoted price or other price of a financial instrument or on its revenue;
   (e) which is not public and which, if it were made public, could have a significant effect on the quoted price or revenue of the financial instrument or other instrument whose value is derived from the financial instrument;

(vi) Inside information is information of a precise nature if:
  (a) it indicates a fact that exists or may reasonably be expected to come into existence in the future; and
  (b) it is specific enough to enable a conclusion to be drawn as to the possible effect of such a fact on the price of the relevant financial instrument or other instruments derived from the financial instrument.

[237] Information which, if it were made public, could have a significant effect on the price or revenue of the financial instrument means information that a reasonable investor would be likely to use as part of the basis of its investment decisions.

[238] Should insider information be disclosed in the process of a due diligence review and be used to the benefit of and by the reviewer or any other third party, such insider information must, without undue delay, be made public by the target company.

[239] An issuer must also (i) maintain a list of entities who can access its inside information, and (ii) provide such a list to the CNB upon its request without undue delay.

ROLE OF THE COURTS

Generally

[240] As in every other democratic country, the role of the courts in the Czech Republic is to provide protection for individual rights. Only a court may decide upon guilt and determine punishment for a criminal offence.

[241] In the Czech Republic, most disputes are resolved in court within civil proceedings, although an increasing number of commercial disputes are resolved through arbitration. The Czech court system is formed by three levels of courts of general jurisdiction and by the Constitutional Court. Cases are assigned to an individual judge on the basis of a schedule allocating court matters, which is set in advance at the beginning of each year. Judges are independent and court rulings are easily enforced either through court execution or via private bailiffs.

[242] There are no apparent tendencies to favour the rights of domestic residents and companies over those of foreigners, or to favour the rights of individuals over those of businesses. The only exception is the area of labour law disputes, where courts tend to rule in favour of employees where possible.

Court System

[243] The structure, functions and powers of the courts of general jurisdiction are regulated by Act No. 6/2002 Coll., on Courts and Judges. This act determines the basic requirements and obligations that must be met by each candidate who runs for the office of judge. Any person who is a citizen of the Czech Republic, is at least thirty years old, has a master's degree in law and fulfils other requirements stipulated by the law may be appointed to the office of judge by the President for an unlimited term. In making their decisions, judges are bound by laws and international treaties that form part of the legal order. Should a court conclude that a law which should be applied in the resolution for the matter is in conflict with the constitution, it shall submit the matter to the Constitutional Court.

[244] The system of general courts is not uniform; depending on the type of dispute the system can be divided into three large branches: (i) civil, (ii) criminal and (iii) administrative.

[245] The general terms of the courts of civil jurisdiction are set out in particular in Act No. 99/1963 Coll., the Civil Procedure Code. This Code deals with individual types of private law disputes, such as disputes arising from civil law, family law, labour law or commercial law. There are no specialised commercial courts dealing with commercial disputes.

[246] The structure of the courts within the civil jurisdiction is as follows:

- (i) Supreme Court seated in Brno;
- (ii) two High Courts located in Prague and Olomouc;
- (iii) regional courts with their seats in regional centres; and
- (iv) district courts.

[247] As a rule, a civil/commercial dispute starts at a district court; however, in certain cases a regional court may act as a Court of First Instance. The Civil Procedure Code lays down an exhaustive list of these cases (e.g., disputes between business corporations, their shareholders or members; disputes arising from intellectual property rights; matters regarding the transformation of business corporations and cooperatives; or cases of financial security and disputes concerning bills of exchange, checks and investment instruments).

[248] In addition, regional courts decide on appeals against the decisions of district courts rendered on the first instance. In cases where the Court of First Instance is the regional court, one of the two High Courts acts as a Court of Appeal.

[249] The Supreme Court is considered as the court of last instance. Its agenda within the civil jurisdiction consists in particular of decisions on (i) extraordinary legal remedies against appellate court decisions and (ii) the recognition of certain rulings made by foreign courts and their enforcement within the Czech Republic.

Costs and Timing

[250] Costs connected to litigation usually include (i) direct expenses incurred by parties in connection with court proceedings, (ii) court fees, (iii) the costs of obtaining evidence, (iv) experts' fees and the costs of translation and interpretation and (v) legal fees.

[251] The court fee for a petition claiming a non-monetary fulfilment is CZK2 000 (approx. EUR76). Where a monetary claim is brought to court, the court fee represents 5% of the claim. The maximum court fee is CZK4.1 m (EUR157 000) for a claim amounting to CZK250 000 000 (approx. EUR9.6 m) and higher.

[252] The general rule is that each party will initially bear its own direct expenses connected to litigation. The court will then rule on the reimbursement of the amounts borne by the parties, depending on who wins the claim. In practice, a party which is successful in litigation is generally awarded all costs reasonably incurred by it in order to successfully bring or defend (as the case may be) the relevant action. If a party is only partially successful, the court generally awards costs on a pro rata basis. In relation to legal fees, however, compensation is awarded according to a special decree, no matter what the agreement between a party and its lawyer was. The difference between the actual fees and awarded fees might thus be enormous.

[253] The main issue, however, is the timing. According to a survey conducted by the Ministry of Justice in 2016, the average time needed to pursue a commercial dispute through the courts is 349 days (from the filing of the initial petition until the day on which the judgment becomes final and enforceable).

Enforceability of Key Contractual Provisions

[254] It is not possible to generalise in respect of how easy or burdensome is to enforce a key contractual provision in court. As will be demonstrated further, some contractual provisions are easier to enforce than others. For example, restrictive covenants and confidentiality constraints might be decided quicker and more easily than warranty and indemnity claims. Generally, whenever a claim for damages is brought to court, it may be expected that the litigation will last much longer than the average time of 349 days.

[255] If an individual's right is breached, the individual may either (i) commence a standard litigation or (ii) file a motion for preliminary injunction.

[256] A preliminary injunction is a kind of interim measure which may be granted by a court to secure an individual claim. In order for a motion for preliminary injunction to be quickly dealt with, it must be demonstrated that there is an urgent need for an interim measure. This condition is usually satisfied when it can be demonstrated that without such a measure, the claimant would be threatened by an objective danger of irreparable damage.

[257] The court has to decide on a motion for preliminary injunction within seven (calendar) days.

[258] If the preliminary injunction is granted by the court, the court usually fixes a deadline (normally thirty days) by which the claimant has to file a standard petition to the court.

[259] If the claimant does not succeed in the litigation, he/she will be obliged to pay compensation to the defendant for damage suffered due to the existence of the preliminary injunction. To secure the payment of such potential compensation, the claimant is obliged to pay a deposit of CZK50 000 (approx. EUR1 900) on the same day that a motion for the preliminary injunction is filed with the court. If the deposit is not paid, the motion for a preliminary injunction shall be rejected by court.

Restrictive Covenants

[260] If a contractual party breaches an obligation under a contract – for example, for a seller not to compete in the future with the business sold by such seller – the buyer may ask the court to order a preliminary injunction or to commence litigation.

[261] In such litigation, the damaged party may claim (i) a ban on the other party competing with the business sold and/or (ii) damages or (iii) payment of a contractual penalty, if so agreed in the sale contract.

[262] The easiest way to proceed is to claim a ban on the other party's competing with the business sold and the payment of any agreed contractual penalty. The court fee would be CZK2 000 (approx. EUR76) for the first claim and 5% of the contractual penalty for any second claim.

[263] Under normal circumstances, it may be expected that the final judgment would be obtained within the average time that it takes for commercial disputes to be resolved.

Confidentiality Constraints

[264] This is a similar situation to those described in paragraphs [260]–[263]. If a contractual party breaches the obligation of confidentiality under a contract, the other party may ask the court to order a preliminary injunction (*see* paragraphs [254]–[259] above) or to commence litigation.

[265] The injured party may claim (i) a ban on the other party disclosing confidential information and/or (ii) damages or (iii) payment of a contractual penalty (if so agreed in the contract).

[266] The easiest way is to claim a ban on the other party disclosing confidential information and the payment of any agreed contractual penalty. The court fee would be CZK2 000 (approx. EUR76) for the first claim and 5% of the contractual penalty for the second claim.

[267] Under normal circumstances, it may be expected that the final judgment would be obtained at around the average time for commercial disputes (*see* paragraphs [250]–[253] above).

Protection of Minority Shareholder Rights

[268] Each shareholder holding shares with a nominal value exceeding its particular share of the registered capital of the company (1%[5], 3%[6], 5%[7] of registered capital) is considered to be a minority shareholder. Compared to other shareholders, these shareholders have a specific right to, for example, (i) request the board of directors to convene a general meeting to discuss issues proposed by them (if the board of directors fails to do so, they may petition a court to authorise them to convene such a general meeting – the costs of this procedure are to be settled by the company); (ii) request the board of directors to include a proposed matter in the agenda of the general meeting; (iii) request the supervisory board to examine the performance of the board of directors in respect of particular matters and inform the shareholders of the results of such an examination. Where the board of directors or supervisory board fails to comply with such requests, the minority shareholders are entitled to file a complaint with the court in the name of the company. Each minority shareholder is also authorised to claim damages in the name of the company against members of the board of directors and members of the supervisory board who have breached their respective obligations resulting from the performance of their office.

[269] The court fee for a court petition authorising a minority shareholder to convene the general meeting will be CZK2 000 (EUR76).

[270] The court fee for a court petition claiming damages would be 5% of the claimed amount.

[271] The law also provides minority shareholders with specific protection in the event of a squeeze-out. In such case, minority shareholders have the right to adequate consideration in cash. The price of the securities must be substantiated and verified by an expert's opinion. If the minority shareholder contests the amount of consideration in court, the court ruling stipulating the amount of such adequate consideration will be binding on all other squeezed-out minority shareholders of a company.

[272] The court fee for a petition by which a minority shareholder claims adequate consideration is CZK2 000 (EUR76) (regardless of the amount in dispute). Such type of dispute is extremely time-consuming and burdensome, since usually, several expert valuations have to be obtained by the court.

[273] Under normal circumstances, the average time for the obtaining of a final judgment would very likely be at least two years.

---

[5] In a company whose registered capital is CZK500 m and higher (approx. EUR19 200 000).

[6] In a company whose registered capital is higher than CZK100 m (approx. EUR3 840 000).

[7] In a company whose registered capital is CZK100 m and lower (approx. EUR3 840 000).

Enforcement of Warranty and Indemnity Claims

[274] If a contractual party breaches the warranty obligation, the recipient of the warranty may typically claim (i) damages or (ii) a reduction in the purchase price. Both concepts differ and require different assertions in the respective petition. Regardless, both types of claim are not only time-consuming but also difficult to prove, since damage/a reduction in the value of contract has to be established prior to the petition being filed. This usually requires that the Claimant obtain an expert valuation on the basis of which the value of the dispute is ascertained. Since the defendant may submit its own expert valuation, the court usually appoints another expert to examine contentious valuations, which increases significantly the costs of the dispute.

[275] The court fee for this type of claim would be 5% of the claimed amount.

[276] The average time for obtaining a final judgment would very likely be under normal circumstances at least two years.

OTHER DISPUTE RESOLUTION MECHANISM

[277] The most frequent dispute resolution mechanism for parties seeking to avoid litigation in court is that of arbitration. In the Czech Republic, it is more common to bring a dispute to the Czech Republic's permanent court of arbitration – the Arbitration Court attached to the Economic Chamber of the Czech Republic and Agricultural Chamber of the Czech Republic (in Czech *Rozhodčí soud při Hospodářské komoře České republiky a Agrární komoře České republiky)* (the *'Court of Arbitration'*).

[278] The Court of Arbitration is based in Prague. It has its own database of arbitrators (currently numbering more than 300). Most of the arbitrators are lawyers who are practising as attorneys and scholars.

[279] Proceedings are usually conducted under its own rules, unless the parties to a dispute have agreed otherwise.

[280] The administrative charges and fees of the arbitrators depend on the value of the dispute. In comparison with other arbitration centres, the Court of Arbitration is one of the least expensive.

MERGER CONTROL / COMPETITION LAW ISSUES

General Introduction

[281] The core rules of Czech competition law, including merger control, are laid down in the Competition Act, which came into effect in 2001. Following the accession of the Czech Republic to the EU on 1 May 2004, the Competition Act had undergone significant changes. Currently, Czech competition law complies with the substantially reformed EU competition law system. The authority in charge of surveying competition law is the Czech Authority for the Protection of Economic Competition (the '*Competition Authority*').

Merger Control Test

[282] A transaction must be notified to the Competition Authority if the following three conditions are satisfied:

(i) the transaction constitutes a concentration;
(ii) at least one of the turnover thresholds is met; and
(iii) the transaction is not subject to notification at the European Commission under Council Regulation No. 139/2004, on the control of concentrations between undertakings (the EU Merger Regulation, '**EUMR**').

Concentration

[283] The following transactions constitute concentrations within the meaning of the Competition Act:

(i) a national or international merger by acquisition or by formation of a new company (amalgamation);
(ii) the acquisition of an enterprise, a part thereof or certain assets by means of an agreement or any other means, including acquisition in a public auction;
(iii) the acquisition of direct or indirect control by one undertaking over another undertaking by:
   - an acquisition of securities (e.g., shares), ownership or membership interests; or
   - the establishment of a (full-function) joint venture; or
   - an agreement (e.g., shareholder agreements, memoranda of association, articles of association, controlling agreements); or
   - any other manner that allows control of the other undertaking.

[284] In contrast, the transactions stipulated above do not constitute a concentration, as defined in the Competition Act, if they take place between undertakings belonging to the same group. Such intra-group consolidations or reorganisations are, therefore, exempt from the notification obligation to the Competition Authority. In addition, certain transactions performed by investment entities (e.g., banks, securities brokers and other financial institutions) do not constitute a concentration and thus are not subject to notification at the Competition Authority.

[285] Two or more concentrations that are mutually conditioned and relate to each other in terms of subject matter, time and entities involved, are considered as a single concentration.

Turnover Thresholds

[286] The second condition is satisfied if one of the following thresholds is met.

[287] The combined net turnover of the concentrating undertakings for the last financial year in the Czech market exceeds CZK1.5 bn (approx. EUR55 147 000) and at least two of the concentrating undertakings each achieved on the Czech market for the last financial year a net turnover of at least CZK250 m (approx. EUR9 191 000); or

[288] The net turnover of:

- at least one of the merging or amalgamating undertakings; or
- the acquired business, a part thereof or the acquired assets; or
- an undertaking in the event of acquisition of its securities (e.g., shares), ownership or membership interest, an agreement, or any other manner which allows the controlling undertaking to control the controlled undertaking; or
- at least one of the undertakings establishing or joining a joint venture.

  for the last financial year on the Czech market exceeds CZK1.5 bn (approx. EUR55 147 000) and the worldwide net turnover of the other concentrating undertaking for the last financial year exceeds CZK1.5 bn (approx. EUR55 147 000).

[289] The Competition Act also provides detailed rules for the calculation of turnovers.

Transaction Subject to European Merger Control

[290] Even though a transaction meets both the conditions stipulated above under paragraphs [16]–[24] (the transaction is a concentration) and [25] of this Chapter 8 (one of the turnover thresholds is met), the transaction is not subject to notification at the Competition Authority if it is subject to notification at the European Commission under the EUMR. In such a case, the so-called one-stop shop principle applies, and the transaction is reviewed by the European Commission only.

Notification Procedure

[291] If all three conditions specified above are met, the transaction is subject to notification at and the approval of the Competition Authority. This section addresses the issues concerning proceedings before the Competition Authority.

Notifying Party

[292] The undertaking(s) that is/are required to file a notification (and is/are responsible for failure to file a notification) is/are as follows:

Type of Concentration	*Notifying Undertaking(s)*
Merger by acquisition or by formation of a new company	All the concentrating undertakings (the notification is to be made jointly)
Acquisition of a business, its substantial part or assets	Undertaking acquiring the business, its substantial part or assets
Acquisition of control over another undertaking	Undertaking acquiring the control
Establishment of joint control over an undertaking (establishment of or joining a joint venture)	All the undertakings establishing the joint control over the undertaking (the notification must be made jointly)

Commencement of the Merger Proceedings

[293] The approval proceedings commence once the Competition Authority receives a completed standard notification or, where applicable, a simplified notification, of the concentration, including all of the required documents. There is no deadline set for submission of the notification. It can be submitted before or after signing of the documents establishing the concentration. However, until the transaction is approved by the Competition Authority, the concentrating undertakings are prohibited from implementing the transaction.

[294] The Competition Authority publishes the commencement of the proceedings in the Commercial Bulletin and on its website. In simplified proceedings, the Competition Authority only publishes the commencement of the proceedings on its website. In the announcement, the Competition Authority also invites third parties to lodge their objections to the concentration.

Notification

[295] There are two possible forms of notification: (i) standard notification and (ii) simplified notification. The latter can be used if the criteria indicating the low impact of the transaction on the market are met.

Standard Notification

[296] In standard notification, the notifying undertakings must provide the Competition Authority with extensive information on the concentration. The documents and other information which must be provided to the Competition Authority are primarily set out in Decree No. 294/2016 Coll., of the Competition Authority (the *'Decree'*). Pursuant to the Decree, the following documents must be submitted:

(a) the completed questionnaire for approval of the concentration;
(b) powers of attorney (if the concentrating undertakings are represented in the proceedings by an attorney-at-law or by another proxy);
(c) extracts of each of the concentrating undertakings from the Commercial Register or, if the undertakings are not Czech entities, from any other similar register;
(d) the undertakings' ownership and control structure charts;
(e) the document(s) establishing the concentration (if available);
(f) the scheme and method of calculation of the turnovers whose levels justify filing of the notification;
(g) the undertakings' annual reports and audited financial statements for the last financial year;
(h) the consolidated financial statements of the undertakings subject to the duty to prepare consolidated financial statements for the last financial year;
(i) reports, analysis, studies and any other similar documents which have been prepared for any member of the Board of Directors or Supervisory Board (or of any other similar corporate body) or for the shareholders' meeting in order to assess the concentration;
(j) an affidavit stipulating that the documents and their translations are true and complete;
(k) evidence of payment of the administrative fee of CZK100 000 (EUR3 675).

[297] The documents must be in Czech. If the originals are not in Czech, their translation must also be submitted. In practice, the Competition Authority does not require the translation of all documents provided that they are available in a commonly used foreign language (such as English).

[298] The core document concerning the notification is the questionnaire referred to in point (i), the contents of which are based on the European Form CO. As a result, the scope of information required by the questionnaire is very extensive.

[299] The Competition Authority has issued detailed guidelines regarding the application of the merger control rules.

Simplified Notification

[300] Simplified notification of a concentration may be filed in the event that:

(a) none of the concentrating undertakings operates on the same relevant market; or
(b) the concentrating undertakings operate on the same relevant market, but their combined share on such market does not exceed 15%, and at the same time, none of the undertakings operates on a market vertically connected to the relevant market on which another undertaking operates, or their share in any such vertically connected market does not exceed 25%; or
(c) an undertaking acquires sole control over a joint venture in which it has so far exercised joint control.

[301] Pursuant to the Decree, the notifying undertakings in the simplified notification procedure must provide the Competition Authority with a completed simplified questionnaire for the approval of the concentration and with the same documents as in the standard procedure.

[302] The Competition Authority has published a Notice on simplified proceedings for the assessment of certain concentrations, which provides further details on the simplified procedure and the conditions for its use.

Stages of the Proceedings

Standard Proceedings

Stages of Proceedings, Deadlines Referrals

[303] There are two possible stages regarding the proceedings. The first stage (commencing once the Competition Authority receives the complete notification) can take up to thirty days, whilst the second stage, if opened, can take up to five months as of the filing of the complete notification.

[304] If the Competition Authority fails to issue a decision within these periods of time, the transaction is deemed to be approved upon expiration of the periods. However, in both stages, the period may be suspended if the Competition Authority requests additional information on the concentration. Such requests automatically interrupt the proceedings and the above-mentioned periods of time do not continue to run until the information requested by the Competition Authority is provided.

[305] The Competition Authority is also given the option of referring a concentration to the European Commission. The Competition Authority is entitled to do so in respect of concentrations affecting trade between Member States and threatening to significantly affect competition within the Member States concerned. If the European Commission accepts the referral, the Competition Authority is obliged to terminate its proceedings.

Phase One

[306] At the beginning of the first phase, the Competition Authority assesses whether the transaction is subject to its approval. If the Competition Authority concludes that the transaction is not subject to its approval, it issues a decision to that effect and terminates the proceedings.

[307] If the transaction is subject to the Competition Authority's approval, the Competition Authority assesses whether the transaction is likely to significantly impede competition, particularly by creating or strengthening a dominant position of the concentrating undertakings.

[308] When assessing the impact of the transaction on competition, the Competition Authority considers, in particular, the necessity of preserving and further developing effective competition, the structure of all markets affected by the transaction, the market shares of the concentrating undertakings in such markets, their economic and financial power, legal and other barriers to entry by other entities into the markets, the alternatives available to suppliers and consumers, the development of supply and demand in the markets, the needs and interests of consumers, research and development, etc. If the combined market share of the concentrating undertakings does not exceed 25% in the relevant market, the concentration is deemed not to substantially lessen competition (unless demonstrated otherwise).

[309] Provided that the transaction does not significantly impede competition, the Competition Authority issues a decision approving the transaction.

[310] On the other hand, if the Competition Authority concludes that the transaction raises serious concerns of a significant impediment of competition, it notifies the notifying undertaking(s) of this fact and the proceedings enter into phase two.

Phase Two

[311] In the second phase, the Competition Authority investigates the market conditions and structure of competition in the relevant markets in greater detail, bearing in mind the need to preserve effective competition.

[312] If the Competition Authority concludes that the transaction would significantly impede competition, then it issues a decision by which it prohibits the transaction.

[313] On the other hand, if the Competition Authority concludes that the transaction does not significantly impede competition, then it issues a decision approving the transaction. The concentrating undertakings may offer (before or during the proceedings) commitments that are proportional to and would entirely eliminate any competition concerns. If the concentrating undertakings offer such commitments after the proceedings have already commenced, the period within which the Competition Authority is required to decide is extended by an additional fifteen days. Alternatively, the Competition Authority is allowed to impose such commitments in its decision, provided that the competitors are willing to accept these commitments.

Simplified Proceedings

[314] When simplified notification is made, the Competition Authority within twenty days either (i) approves the concentration by means of a simplified positive decision or (ii) finds that it needs additional information in order to assess the concentration and issues a request that the party/parties to the proceedings submit a standard notification. In the latter case, a standard procedure as described above follows.

[315] If the Competition Authority fails to issue a decision within the twenty-day period, the transaction is deemed to have been approved upon expiry of this period.

Implementation of the Transaction

Mandatory Suspension of Implementation

[316] Pursuant to the Competition Act, until the transaction is approved by the Competition Authority, the concentrating undertakings are prohibited from implementing the transaction. In particular, the concentrating undertakings must avoid determining or influencing each other's competitive conduct (e.g., exercising voting rights, adopting new business plans or taking any other action which may materially affect their businesses or operations). However, this does not apply to concentrations in the form of takeover offers or a series of transactions with publicly traded securities resulting in acquiring control from different entities, provided that the notification is made without undue delay and the voting rights connected with such securities are not exercised.

Application for an Exemption

[317] The concentrating undertakings may apply to the Competition Authority, either along with filing the standard form notification or during the standard notification proceedings, for an exemption from prohibition on the implementation of the transaction if there is a serious risk that they or other third entities will incur significant damage or any other serious detriment.

[318] The Competition Authority must render a decision thereon within thirty days of the submission of the application. If the Competition Authority fails to render the decision in this period, the application is deemed approved. The Competition Authority may also request additional information necessary for assessing the application for the exemption and the time period between the delivery of such a request and its fulfilment is not included in the thirty-day period.

[319] If the Competition Authority grants the exemption, it may require fulfilment of certain commitments which it considers necessary for preserving effective competition. It may also grant the exemption only partially – with respect to certain legal acts which are part of the notified concentration.

Consequences

[320] If the Competition Authority discovers that the concentrating undertakings implemented the transaction without filing the notification or prior to its approval, it is authorised, in addition to imposing the fines described below, to order the undertakings to 'demerge', i.e., to sell the shares, transfer the business, cancel any relevant agreements and/or adopt other measures necessary to restore effective competition in the relevant market.

Competition Authority's Authorisations

Right to Information

[321] It is generally in the undertakings' interest to provide the Competition Authority with sufficient information on the transaction so that the proceedings can proceed smoothly and as quickly as possible.

[322] In addition, the Competition Authority is also authorised to request the undertakings to provide it with additional information. Failure to provide the Competition Authority with such information may lead to an interruption of the proceedings. The Competition Authority is also authorised to impose severe fines for failure to submit such information.

Power to Investigate

[323] The Competition Authority has extensive powers to investigate undertakings in the Czech Republic, e.g., to enter business premises and land, to examine business books or records and make copies or extracts, ask for explanations or seal off any business premises and books or records for the inspection period. Upon prior authorisation by a court, the Competition Authority may even inspect private premises, including the homes of directors, managers and other members of staff of the respective undertakings.

Fines and Remedial Measures

Fines

[324] The Competition Authority may impose severe fines for breaching merger control regulations. These fines may amount up to:

(i) CZK10 m (approx. EUR368 000) or up to 10% of the net turnover achieved in the last financial year in the event of a breach of the prohibition on implementation of the transaction without approval or before the approval of the Competition Authority is granted, or for non-compliance with the Competition Authority's order to 'demerge' or an unenforceable decision of the Competition Authority.

(ii) CZK300 000 (approx. EUR11 000) or up to 1% of the net turnover achieved in the last financial period for failing to submit information requested by the Competition Authority, submission of incorrect, incomplete or false information, or any other refusal to cooperate with the Competition Authority or for breaching the seal affixed by the Competition Authority. Such a fine may be imposed repeatedly up to a total amount of CZK10 m (approx. EUR368 000) or up to a total amount equal to 10% of the net turnover achieved in the previous financial year.

Remedial Measures

[325] The Competition Authority may, in addition to the above fines, impose remedial measures to be taken by the undertakings and may set reasonable deadlines for their implementation. The Competition Authority may, e.g., order the undertakings to 'demerge' or to adopt other measures necessary to restore effective competition on the relevant market.

TAXATION ASPECTS

Nature of the Tax Regime

[326] The Czech jurisdiction can be described as transparent. The tax rules are complex; historically, they were not enforced aggressively. In the past years, however, a shift to a more aggressive tax collection and aimed audits is noticeable.

Liability to Tax

[327] Corporate income tax payers comprise: (a) a legal entity, (b) a government branch of government, (c) a mutual fund under the Act Regulating Investment Companies and Investment Funds, (d) a sub-fund of a joint-stock company with variable registered capital under the Act Regulating Investment Companies and Investment Funds, (e) a fund of a pension company (meaning a fund managed by a pension company under the Act Regulating Pension Savings and under the Act Regulating Supplementary Pension Savings, (f) a trust fund under the Civil Code, and (g) a unit that is a payer under the law of the state under which it was founded or established.

[328] Tax payers comprise both Czech tax residents or tax non-residents.

[329] Czech tax residents (companies with their registered seat or place of management in the Czech Republic) are taxed on their worldwide income. Czech tax non-residents are taxed only on their income from Czech sources (e.g., dividends, interest, royalties) while respecting the provisions of applicable double taxation treaties. The Czech Republic is party to 88 (as of 31 January 2019) double taxation treaties. Most of the treaties are based on the 1977 OECD (Organisation for Economic Co-operation and Development) Model Convention.

[330] The income generated from activities undertaken through a permanent establishment shall be considered as constituting income of a foreign company from sources in the Czech Republic. Such income is subject to 19% corporate income tax in the Czech Republic. Income gained from services provided from outside the Czech Republic should not be attributable to the Czech permanent establishment.

Corporate Tax Rate

[331] The corporate tax rate for the tax year 2019 is 19%; no change to this rate is planned for now.

[332] The tax base is the profit (or loss) figure reported according to Czech Accounting Standards, adjusted for non-deductible expenses and non-taxable income, as set out in the Czech Income Taxes Act.

Taxes on Capital Gains

[333] Profit on the sale of shares/an ownership interest realised by a Czech corporate resident is included in the annual corporate income tax return. A loss is generally non-tax-deductible.

[334] Profit on the sale of shares/an ownership interest in a Czech company realised by a non-Czech tax resident is taxable in the Czech Republic. The buyer must withhold a tax advance from a purchase price payment made to a resident outside the EU or the European Economic Area. This tax advance is then treated as a tax prepayment in respect of the non-Czech-resident seller. After the end of the year, the non-Czech-resident seller is obliged to file a Czech tax return, declare any capital gains (profit) in the tax return and pay the tax. The tax advance previously deducted can be set off against the tax liability declared in the tax return. However, taxation is usually eliminated by a double taxation treaty.

CFC Rules

[335] Rules for the taxation of controlled foreign companies (CFC) has been implemented into the Czech tax law according to the EU Anti-Avoidance Directive (ATAD) as of 2019. Selected income of a foreign controlled company (such as income from dividends, interest and royalties) shall be part of the tax base of the Czech controlling company that holds directly or indirectly more than 50% of the share of the controlled company or that participates in more than half of its profit or voting rights. The rule shall be applied if the foreign company does not carry out substantial business activity and its taxation abroad is lower than half of its potential tax obligation in the Czech Republic.

Value Added Tax (VAT) or Sales Taxes or Other Taxes on Revenue/Sales

[336] VAT law has been harmonised with the relevant EU Directives since 1 May 2004.

[337] The standard VAT rate is 21%, the first reduced VAT rate is 15% and the second reduced VAT rate is 10%. A company is generally obliged to register for VAT if its turnover for VAT purposes during the previous twelve calendar months exceeds CZK1 m (approx. EUR38 500). An entity may also be obliged to register for VAT if it purchases goods from other EU Member States or certain services from abroad. Upon the acquisition of an enterprise from a seller who is VAT-registered, the buyer is also obliged to register for VAT, unless already registered. Voluntary VAT registration is possible. VAT group registration is possible.

Stamp Duties or Other Taxes on Land Transactions

[338] A sale of real estate is subject to real estate transfer tax at 4% of the sale price or expert's valuation (whichever is higher). The buyer is primarily liable for the payment of the real estate transfer tax.

Other Taxes on Land or Real Estate

[339] Companies and individuals who own property as at 1 January of the current year are subject to real estate property tax in that year. Two separate taxes are payable: tax on land and tax on buildings.

[340] The tax base of plots of land (with the exception of arable land, hop fields, vineyards, gardens and orchards, meadowlands and pastures, commercial forests and ponds) is the actual area of the plot of land in square meters.

Capital Duties or Other Duties on Share Capital

[341] In the Czech Republic capital duty is not levied on share capital.

Business Rates

[342] No special business rates are levied in the Czech Republic.

Taxes Imposed on Employers (e.g., PAYE and Social Security Obligations)

[343] Social security contributions are payable to the Czech Social Security Office. Health insurance contributions are payable to the Czech Health Insurance Company with which the employee is insured.

[344] The employer contributes 9% of the employee's gross income to the employee's health insurance and 25% of the employee's gross income to the social security system. The annual basis for the calculation of social security contributions is capped at a multiple of forty-eight times the officially published average national monthly salary (i.e., the annual cap on the gross salary is CZK1 569 552 (approx. EUR60 400) for the year 2019). After the income cap is reached, no further contributions have to be made. The cap on health care contributions was revoked in 2013 and such contributions are not capped.

Customs and Excise Duties

[345] Custom duties can be levied on imports from countries outside the EU. Excise duty is levied on 'mineral oils' (i.e., fuel), spirits, beer, wine and tobacco. Rates of the excise duty differ according to the kind of goods.

R&D Costs

[346] Certain R&D cost may be claimed as a special tax allowance.

Tax Consolidation. Group Relief of Gains and Losses

[347] Tax losses can be carried forward and set off against future profits in the subsequent five years. Companies within the same group are generally not able to transfer losses to each other for tax purposes, since a tax loss is not transferable to another entity.

Tax Considerations Arising on M&A Transactions

[348] Profit on a sale performed by a private individual is exempt from income tax after a minimum holding period of three years (in the case of securities) or five years (in the case of shares). In other cases, the profit is reported in an annual tax return and is subject to personal income tax.

[349] Profit on a sale realised by a Czech corporate resident is included in the annual corporate income tax return unless the tax exemption under the EU Parent-Subsidiary Directive applies. A loss is generally non-tax-deductible.

[350] Profit on the sale of shares/an ownership interest in a Czech company realised by a non-Czech tax resident is taxable in the Czech Republic unless the tax exemption under the EU Parent-Subsidiary Directive applies. The buyer must withhold a tax advance from a purchase price payment made to a resident of a state that is outside the EU or the European Economic Area. However, taxation is usually eliminated by a double taxation treaty.

[351] The acquisition price of shares is tax-deductible for the buyer upon the disposal of the shares. No 'step-up' can be achieved in the tax base of the underlying assets owned by the target, since the transfer does not affect the acquisition costs.

[352] Deduction of tax losses carried forward by a transferred company is restricted. If the transfer of shares leads to a substantial change in the shareholder structure (generally a change affecting more than 25% of the capital or voting rights) the company can deduct tax losses only if 80% of its revenues are generated from the same activities as those that the company conducted in the year in which it incurred the loss.

[353] Costs related to the holding of shares/an ownership interest (e.g., interest on acquisition financing) are non-tax-deductible. The tax deductibility of costs may, however, be achieved by appropriate acquisition structuring and a subsequent transformation.

[354] Costs related to the holding of an ownership interest in a subsidiary, which were non-tax-deductible in respect of the parent company during the holding period may generally increase the acquisition price of an ownership interest during the sale. Given that the acquisition price is regarded as a tax-deductible cost in respect of the parent company, the tax deductibility of costs which arose prior to the sale (and which were non-tax-deductible) is achieved during the sale unless the profit on the sale is tax exempt.

Transfer Taxes

[355] The transfer of shares is not subject to VAT, real estate transfer tax or any other taxes or stamp duties.

Transfer of Tax Liabilities

[356] The buyer 'inherits' the tax history of the acquired company, including its latent tax liabilities. Some companies use deferred payments or retentions; however, it is not commonly used as an instrument for mitigating transaction risks.

[357] The Czech Tax Administration Act stipulates a general tax assessment period of three years, starting on the last day for filing the regular tax return. In addition, those years in which a corporate income tax loss was recorded may be audited within the extended period – i.e., the same period as for the years in which the loss might be utilised. Given that the tax loss may be utilised in the five following years, for the tax loss years the period is three plus five years. The period starts anew if the Tax Authority initiates a tax audit of the tax payer. The period might be automatically prolonged by certain actions taken by the tax payer, e.g., filing an additional tax return during the last year of the period. The maximum time limitation is ten years from the last day for the filing the regular tax return. The statute of limitations in respect of already-assessed tax receivables is six years from the last day for filing the regular tax return; this period is extendable by a tax administrator or the courts up to the maximum statute of limitation period of twenty years.

[358] Any gain arising upon the sale of assets (i.e., the difference between the sales price and the tax residual value) is included to the tax base of the company and subject to general corporate income tax at 19%.

[359] The gain can be offset against any existing tax losses from previous tax periods.

[360] In practice, the tax residual value of the developed property is often lower than its fair market value. For an asset deal it is possible for the buyer to recognise the 'fair value' purchase price as the basis for tax depreciation purposes. A 'step-up' in the tax base of assets is thus achieved, as the assets will be depreciated from the acquisition price recorded in the buyer's accounts as if they had been newly acquired. Certain assets, such as land, are excluded from depreciation.

[361] Any tax losses realised by the seller and related to the transferred assets may not be transferred to the buyer.

Real Estate Transfer Tax

[362] The transfer of real estate is subject to a real estate transfer tax of 4%. The tax base is either the agreed purchase price or the transfer value according to an expert valuation under Czech valuation law, whichever is higher. The taxpayer is generally the buyer.

VAT

[363] The transfer of movable assets, a building land, and associated rights is subject to VAT. A transfer of real estate (except for building land) executed five years or more after the issuance of final building approval or the first use of the buildings is exempt from VAT. If the approval of the real estate changes to that of another usage, the period runs from the beginning. In most cases, however, the seller may opt for the VAT to be charged on the real estate transfer. A transfer of receivables is generally not subject to VAT.

[364] If it is registered for VAT, a buyer is entitled to claim the deduction of VAT charged by the seller in accordance with the general provisions of the VAT Act.

Transfer of Tax Liabilities

Sale of Assets

[365] Tax liabilities that have arisen in relation to the seller's enterprise do not pass to the buyer as a result of the acquisition of assets.

[366] The sale price of assets is determined by the market and business negotiation. In the case of a sale of assets, a company will record the acquired assets in its accounting under 'purchase prices'.

Merger

[367] The merger process is tax-neutral from the corporate income tax point of view. The receiving company is entitled to take over those items that are deductible from the tax base which relate to the transferred business and to which the transferring company had become entitled (but chose not to utilise) – (e.g., tax losses, R&D relief, etc.). It is not possible to ask the tax authorities for a binding opinion.

[368] The deduction of tax losses carried forward by a transferred company is restricted. If the transfer of shares leads to a substantial change in the shareholder structure (generally a change affecting more than 25% of the capital or voting rights) the company can deduct tax losses only if 80% of its revenues are generated from the same activities as those that the company conducted in the year in which it incurred the loss.

[369] Some companies use deferred payments or retentions; however, it is not commonly used as instrument for mitigating transaction risks.

[370] Costs related to the acquisition of shares, such as legal, tax and property advisory costs, are generally not deductible. They should generally be capitalised as part of the acquisition costs of the shares.

Structuring the Investment: Withholding Taxes

Dividends Paid to Foreign Corporate/Group Shareholders

[371] The distribution of profits/dividends is subject to withholding tax levied at a rate of 15%. Withholding tax can be reduced or eliminated on the basis of double taxation treaties, or, if payable to a parent company in an EU Member State, eliminated under the conditions set out in the EU Parent-Subsidiary Directive.

Dividends Paid to Foreign Individual Shareholders

[372] The distribution of profits/dividends is subject to withholding tax levied at a rate of 15%. withholding tax can be reduced or eliminated on the basis of double taxation treaties.

Dividends Received from Foreign Subsidiaries/Affiliates

[373] Profits/dividends received from a foreign country are included in a separate tax base and are subject to tax levied at a rate of 15%. The tax previously deducted can be set off against the tax liability declared in the Czech tax return.

[374] Profits/dividends received by a Czech parent company from a foreign subsidiary in an EU Member State may be tax exempt under the EU Parent-Subsidiary Directive.

Interest Paid to Foreign Corporate/Group Shareholders or Affiliates

[375] Interest paid to a non-Czech tax resident is generally subject to 15% withholding tax unless provided for otherwise in a double taxation treaty. Furthermore, the withholding tax on interest charged between related entities can generally be eliminated under the conditions set out in the EU Interest-Royalties Directive.

[376] Since 2013, withholding tax of 35% has been levied on the most types of incomes if they are paid to a tax resident of a state with which the Czech Republic has no double taxation treaty or tax information exchange agreement.

Interest Received from Foreign Corporate/Group Shareholders or Affiliates

[377] Such income is subject to 19% corporate income tax in the Czech Republic.

Intellectual Property (IP) Royalties Paid to Foreign Corporate/Group Shareholders or Affiliates

[378] The Czech Income Taxes Act defines compensation paid by a Czech tax resident to a tax non-resident for the right to use intellectual property as income subject to Czech corporate income tax. This income is subject to a withholding tax of 15%. Withholding tax can be reduced or eliminated on the basis of double taxation treaties. Furthermore, the withholding tax on royalties charged between related entities can generally be eliminated under the conditions set out in the EU Interest-Royalties Directive.

Intellectual Property (IP) Royalties Received from Foreign Corporate/Group Shareholders or Affiliates

[379] Such income is subject to 19% corporate income tax in the Czech Republic.

Management or Consultancy Fees Paid to Foreign Corporate/Group Shareholders or Affiliates

[380] Fees for management or consultancy services performed in the territory of the Czech Republic and paid to corporate/group shareholders within the European Union are either not liable to withholding tax or give rise to the creation of a Czech permanent establishment. Withholding tax of up to 35% applies if paid to a tax resident of a country with no double tax treaty or tax information exchange agreement with the Czech Republic.

Payments to Non-residents in Respect of the Purchase or Renting of Immovable Property

[381] Payments to non-residents in respect of the purchase or renting of immovable property located in the Czech Republic are in general subject to either 15% Czech personal income tax or 19% Czech corporate income tax, depending on the non-resident's status.

Double Tax Treaties

[382] The Czech Republic is party to 88 (as at 31 January 2019) double taxation treaties. Most of the treaties are based on the 1977 OECD Model Tax Convention (for details, please *see* the OECD Commentary on the Model Convention). Although the Commentary is not legally binding, it is normally used by Czech tax authorities for the interpretation of double tax treaties.

Debt Financing

Are Finance Costs Associated with the Acquisition Generally Deductible

[383] In the case of an asset deal, the interest on acquisition financing is generally tax-deductible. However, new rules restricting the deductibility of exceeding borrowing costs are implemented into the corporate income tax legislation under the ATAD as of 2019. Further, if the financing is provided by a related entity, the restrictions set out in the transfer pricing rule and the thin capitalisation rule apply. In the case of a share deal, the costs related to the holding of shares/an ownership interest (e.g., interest on acquisition financing) are non-tax-deductible. The tax deductibility of costs may, however, be achieved by appropriate acquisition structuring and a subsequent transformation under certain conditions.

Deductibility of Exceeding Borrowing Costs

[384] The financial expenses related to received loans, credits, and also leasing and derivatives (including relating exchange rate differences and capitalised interest) that exceed possible associated financial revenues are tax-deductible up to the amount of CZK80 m (approx. EUR3 m) or up to 30% of the tax revenue before deducting interest, tax and depreciation and amortisations (EBITDA) if the latter amount is higher. Borrowing costs exceeding the above thresholds shall be considered tax non-deductible; however, they may be deducted in the following years.

[385] The rule shall be applied in tax periods starting after 1 April 2019 and covers also financial instruments provided by unrelated parties (such as bank loans) irrespective of the date when the relevant financial instrument was entered into force. It shall be applied by almost all entities with the exception of selected financial institutions and entities that are not members of any group.

Thin Capitalisation

[386] Thin capitalisation rules apply in the Czech Republic and may limit the tax deductibility of interest payments and other related financial costs related to debt financing from related parties.

[387] The deductibility of interest and financing costs in respect of third-party financing is not restricted under the Czech thin capitalisation rules. Also, if there is a back-to-back arrangement when a third-party debt is guaranteed or secured by related-party credit or a deposit granted to the lender, the thin capitalisation rules also apply.

[388] The debt/equity ratio is 4:1 – i.e., interest payments and related financial costs relating to the portion of a related-party debt financing that exceed four times the borrower's equity are non-tax-deductible for the borrower.

[389] The debt is calculated as the average of daily debt balance amounts, rounded to two decimal places. For the calculation of equity, a weighted average shall be used. The equity for thin capitalisation purposes includes (i) registered (share) capital, and (ii) other equity accounts, typically: retained earnings, other capital funds, statutory funds, share premium.

[390] Any interest and related financial costs exceeding the ratio shall be considered as non-tax-deductible.

Transfer Pricing

[391] Prices between related parties must be set at fair market value (the 'arm's-length' principle) for tax purposes. 'Related parties' include entities or individuals related by capital (directly or indirectly, via participation in capital or voting rights of 25% or more) or in another way (e.g., via management or control or connected persons).

[392] Generally, OECD transfer pricing guidelines are to be applied when determining whether prices between related parties conform to the arm's-length principle. It is not explicitly required by Czech tax legislation to have written transfer pricing documentation in advance, it is, however, very strongly recommended. A company has to be able to prove to the tax authorities that the arms' length principle has been observed upon request during a tax audit.

[393] Interest charged between related parties must also be at arm's length.

EMPLOYMENT CONSIDERATIONS

Labour Law and Employment Considerations

General Introduction

[394] Employment in the Czech Republic is regulated by various acts, of which the most important are Act No. 262/2006 Coll., the Labour Code (the '*Labour Code*'), Act No. 435/2004 Coll., on Employment (the '*Employment Act*'), Act No. 251/2005 Coll., on Work Inspection (the '*Work Inspection Act*') and Act No. 2/1991 Coll., on Collective Bargaining (the '*Collective Bargaining Act*').

Employment Contracts

General Concept

[395] Although the previous rigid concept of employment law has been superseded, employment law in the Czech Republic is still very employee-protective.

[396] Most provisions in the Labour Code are mandatory; however, parties to employment contracts may deviate from the Labour Code where the Labour Code does not so prohibit or agree on a different arrangement if the wording of the Labour Code does not prescribe anything specific.

Obligatory Contents

[397]

(i) A valid employment contract must contain at least the following:
  (a) the type of work in which the employee will be engaged;
  (b) the place where the work will be performed (municipality, organisational unit or other specified place); and
  (c) the date on which the employee starts work.

(ii) An employment contract must be concluded in writing. Even though a lack of written form does not render an employment contract invalid, an employer may be penalised by the relevant Work Inspectorate for a breach of its obligation to conclude written employment contracts with a fine of up to CZK10 000 000 (approx. EUR37 000). Work Inspectorates are regional governmental authorities that supervise the fulfilment of the obligations arising from the labour law regulations.

(iii) In addition to the above, parties to an employment contract may agree on other conditions (e.g., that the employee be required to undertake business travel, that the employee not engage in competition with the employer after termination of the employment contract, etc.).

(iv) If an employment contract does not contain information on the essential terms of the employment, the employer is required to notify the employee of such terms in writing at the latest within one month of commencement of the employment. The notification must contain detailed information on the following: the identity of the parties, a description of the work, the place of work, holiday entitlement, termination notice periods, the amount of salary and the method of its payment, the weekly working hours and collective agreements. Non-compliance with this requirement does not render an employment contract invalid, but may result in penalties of up to CZK300 000 (approx. EUR11 000) being imposed on the employer by the appropriate Work Inspectorate.

(v) Employment may be part-time or full-time and may be entered into for a fixed or an unlimited term. Employment is presumed to be entered into for an unlimited term unless the contract provides for a specific term.

(vi) Trial period
An employment contract may provide for a trial period lasting three months, unless a shorter period has been agreed upon. For managers, such trial period can last six months. The trial period must be agreed upon in writing in order to be valid, and it may not be extended. During the trial period, the employment may be terminated for any reason or without any reason by either party. In such case, no notice period is required and the employment is terminated on day of the delivery of the notice in writing. A

trial period must not be agreed longer than half of the agreed duration of the employment relationship

(vii) Pensions

Pensions in the Czech Republic are based on mandatory pension schemes to which both (employers and employees) contribute (i.e., employers do not establish separate private pension funds).

Non-competition

Non-competition During Employment

[398] During employment, an employee may engage in gainful activity identical to the employer's scope of business only with the employer's prior written consent. The employer may revoke such consent in writing at any time. If the employee breaches this obligation, the employer can claim damages resulting from the employee's breach, or can take steps to terminate the employment on the grounds of the employee's breach of working discipline.

Non-competition after Termination of Employment

[399]

(i) Parties to the employment contract may agree on a non-competition agreement, under which the employee undertakes not to engage in any gainful activities which would compete with the employer's business activities, for a period of up to one year following the termination of the employee's employment.

(ii) The non-competition agreement can only be concluded with those employees who have access to sensitive information or know-how, the use of which in competition against the employer after the end of their employment could harm the employer. The employer must undertake to provide the employee with compensation in the minimum amount of one half of the employee's average monthly salary for each month of compliance with the non-competition obligations.

(iii) The non-competition arrangement may be set out in a separate agreement, but more often it is a clause in an employment contract. It must be made in writing and must comply with the above conditions, otherwise it is invalid. The employer can withdraw from the non-competition agreement (or clause) only before the end of the relevant employment, provided that such entitlement to withdraw is stipulated in the law or in the agreement between the parties (including relevant reasons for such withdrawal).

Fixed-Term Employment Contracts

Restrictions

[400]

(i) The Labour Code contains restrictions on employers regarding the conclusion of an employment contract for a fixed term.

(ii) Fixed-term employment between the same parties can last for a maximum period of three years from the date of its commencement. Such period of fixed-term employment can be repeated two times, and each time for a maximum period of three years. An extension of the term of employment is considered to have the same effect as a repetition of the employment for a fixed-term period (i.e., an employment concluded for a period of up to three years can be extended two times, each time by a period of up to three years). This restriction also applies to any and all additional fixed-term employment agreed during the stated period between the same parties. On the other hand, the restriction does not apply if three years have elapsed since the termination of the previous fixed-term employment.

(iii) The Labour Code sets out three exceptions to the above-mentioned restriction. The first exception applies whenever a special legal regulation presumes that an employment can last only for a fixed term. The second exception applies to employees hired by a work agency for the purpose of being allocated to another employer. And the third exemption applies if on the employer's part there are serious operational reasons, or reasons arising from the special nature of the work, which would make it unreasonable to require an employer to propose establishing an employment relationship for an indefinite term with the employee who is to perform such work, provided that any alternative procedure followed is appropriate to such reasons and that the written agreement of the employer with the trade union sets out: (a) a detailed specification of such reasons, (b) the rules of the alternative procedure followed by the employer in contracting and repeating employment law relationships for a fixed term, (c) the group of the employer's employees to whom the different procedure shall apply, and (d) the period for which such agreement is made. The written agreement with the trade union may be substituted by an internal regulation only when there is no trade union active at the employer.

Consequences

[401] If an employer concludes fixed-term employment with an employee without the conditions stated in paragraph [400] being fulfilled and the employee notifies the employer in writing prior to the expiry of the agreed term that it insists on continuing the employment, then it follows that the employment is agreed for an indefinite period. A petition for a ruling on whether the above conditions have been fulfilled or not can be submitted to a court by either party at the latest up to two months from the date on which the employment was due to end with the expiry of the agreed period.

Employment of Top-Level Managers

[402] The Czech Labour Code does not distinguish between the employment of 'ordinary employees' and managers in 'lower positions' and employment of 'top-level managers'. All of these categories are employed under employment agreements. However, the definition of a top-level manager is important with respect to the dismissal/resignation of top-level managers.

Defining a Top-Level Manager

[403] A top-level manager under the Labour Code is an employee who fulfils both of the following conditions:

(i) S/he is considered to be a manager (i.e., an employee who is entrusted with the management of individuals, and is authorised to determine and assign work to subordinates as well as to organise, manage and supervise work and give binding instructions); and

(ii) S/he is in a top position within the employer's operations, being directly subordinated to:

   (a) the employer's executive body (the board of directors of a joint-stock company or the executive director of a limited liability company); or

   (b) another manager who is directly subordinated to the employer's executive body,

   but only if s/he has another subordinated manager (rather than just 'ordinary employees') below him/her – i.e., if there are (at least) three levels of managers under the executive body, only the top two are considered to be top-level managers. The parties may also agree in the employment contract that the employee's position is considered to be a managerial position, provided that such agreement is reasonable.

Dismissal or Resignation of Top-Level Managers

[404] Since top-level managers are considered to be regular employees, no special rules regarding the termination of their office shall apply. The employment of top-level managers may be terminated as described below. Unlike the heads of state authorities, top-level managers cannot be recalled unless it was previously agreed (provided that it was also agreed that he or she may resign from their office).

[405] The only requirement for the recall or resignation to be valid is that it must be in writing and delivered to the other party. However, such recall or resignation only terminates a top-level manager's office as a top-level manager and has no effect on his/her employment with the company. The employer must agree with the former top-level manager on his/her subsequent placement within the company. If there are no vacancies available or the top-level manager refuses a vacancy, it is regarded as constituting a reason for giving notice under paragraph [408] (iii). A top-level manager is entitled to severance pay only if s/he was dismissed from his/her position because the position ceased to exist as a result of an organisational change.

Termination of the Employment Contract

[406] Employment may be terminated by agreement, by notice or by immediate cancellation. Fixed-term employment also ends with the expiry of the period for which the employment was agreed (i.e., a fixed-term employment could also be terminated by any of the means stipulated below).

Termination by Agreement

[407] Employment may be terminated by agreement at any time and for any reason. The agreement must be in writing. If the employee so requests, the agreement must state the reasons for termination.

Termination by Notice

[408]

(i) Employment may be terminated by notice given by either the employer or the employee. The notice must be in writing and delivered to the other party; otherwise it is not taken into account. Whereas the employer may only serve notice on the employee for certain reasons prescribed by the Labour Code and the notice must clearly set out the reason for the termination, the employee may serve notice at will without stating the reason for termination.

(ii) A minimum notice period of two months is set for both employees and employers. The employer and the employee may agree on a longer notice period; however, such notice period must be the same for both parties. The notice period runs from the first day of the calendar month following the month in which the notice was delivered. In the event that the employee serves notice for reasons connected to the transfer of his employment relationship, the employment terminates no later than on the day preceding such transfer.

(iii) The employer may serve notice on the employee only for the following reasons, which must exist at the time when notice is given – otherwise the notice is invalid:

(a) the employer, or a part of it, winds up its business activities;

(b) the employer, or a part of it, relocates;

(c) the employee becomes redundant as a result of the decision made by the employer or its competent body to change its business or commercial objectives;
(d) if, according to a medical certificate, the employee is not allowed to perform his/her current work;
(e) if, according to a medical certificate, the employee has lost, for the long term, his/her capability to perform his/her current work due to his/her state of health;
(f) if the employee does not meet the prerequisites for an individual undertaking the type of work the employee is performing;
(g) if the employee seriously or constantly breaches working discipline (i.e., obligations that arise from his/her employment contract, from the internal rules of the employer or from other regulations that govern the employment of that employee), if there are reasons due to which the employment can be terminated immediately; or
(h) if the employee commits a gross breach of a 'temporary unfitness to work regime due to sickness' (in Czech: '*režim dočasně práce neschopného zaměstnance*') during the first two weeks of such regime.

(iv) Under paragraph [408] (iii) (a) to [408] (iii) (c), the employee becomes redundant as a result of the employer's decision to change its goals or to reduce the number of employees for the purpose of increasing work efficiency.

(v) The reason in paragraph [408](iii) (d) and [408] (iii) (e) concerns the state of the employee's health. Here, the employer serves notice because, in the opinion of a medical expert or in line with a decision of a state health administration authority or a state social security authority, the employee's health is such that the employee has suffered a long-term loss of capacity to perform the work s/he had been doing until that time.

(vi) The reason in paragraph [408] (iii) (f) deals with the case in which an employee does not meet the prerequisites for the performance of the agreed work. This reason may be applied:
- if the employee does not meet the legal requirements for the performance of the agreed work (e.g., a professional driver has a driver's licence that has been suspended);
- if the employee does not meet the standards of performance set by the employer, without this being the fault of the employer; or
- if the employee's work performance is unsatisfactory, provided that the employer has, within the last twelve months, requested the employee in writing to remedy such deficiency and given the employee a reasonable period in which to remedy such deficiency, and the employee has failed to do so. Without this request the termination notice is invalid.

(vii) The reason in paragraph [408] (iii) (g) concerns an employee's violation of working discipline. In order for the employer to terminate employment, the violation must be caused by the employee – that is to say, the employee has to engage in wilful or negligent behaviour. The employee must have committed a serious violation of working discipline (e.g., drinking alcohol at work). Notice may be given for a less serious violation (e.g., late arrival for work) which has reoccurred if, during the last six months, the employee has been warned in writing of the possibility of his/her being dismissed in connection with said violation of working discipline. A reoccurring violation is usually interpreted to mean a violation that occurs a total of three times.

(viii) The employer may dismiss the employee due to misconduct only within a period of two months from the day on which it learned of the grounds for such dismissal, but no later than one year after the day on which these grounds arose.

(ix) Employers should be cautious when using the termination reason set out in paragraph [408] (iii) (h) as the case law interpreting it is still limited. There are not sufficient court rulings providing a specific guidance as to what is meant by a gross breach in such a case and what evidence should be obtained by an employer in order to avoid any risk of the termination being invalid.

(x) The law provides a protection period during which the employer may not serve notice on the employee. This protection applies to employees who are pregnant, on parental leave, on sickness leave, who permanently care for a child younger than three years or who are on military or civil service. The prohibition on serving notice does not apply if notice is served due to the organisational reasons mentioned under paragraph [408] (iii) (a) and [408] (iii) (b) or due to a violation of work discipline (*see* paragraph [408] (iii) (g)).

Immediate Cancellation by the Employer

[409]

(i) An employer may cancel employment immediately only in exceptional cases, and only for the following reasons:
  (a) the employee was definitely and validly sentenced for an intentional criminal act to an unconditional period of imprisonment of at least one year or for an intentional criminal act committed in connection with its work to an unconditional period of imprisonment of at least six months; or
  (b) the employee commits a gross breach of working discipline (e.g., physically assaults another employee).

(ii) Time limitation described in paragraph [408] (viii) applies also to immediate cancellation of employment due to a gross breach of working discipline.

(iii) An employer may not terminate employment by immediate cancellation in relation to an employee who is pregnant or an employee who permanently cares for a child younger than three years of age. The employer may terminate employment with such employees, provided that there are grounds for immediate cancellation, by giving two months' notice. However, an employee on the first twenty eight weeks of parental leave (thirty seven weeks in the case of a single mother or a mother of two or more children born at the same time) is protected against any form of termination.

Immediate Cancellation by the Employee

[410]

(i) An employee may cancel employment immediately only in exceptional cases, and only for the following reasons:
  (a) in the opinion of a medical expert, s/he cannot continue to perform the work specified in the employment contract without a serious threat to his/her health and the employer has not transferred him/her to another position or alternative work within fifteen days of having been notified to that effect; or
  (b) the employer is in default with payment of the employee's salary for more than fifteen days.

(ii) The employee may immediately cancel employment only within a period of two months from the day on which s/he learnt of the grounds for immediate cancellation, but no later than one year after the day on which these grounds arose.

(iii) An employee who immediately terminates his/her employment shall be entitled to compensation for salary or public sector pay from the employer in the amount of the average earnings for the time corresponding to the duration of the notice period.

Collective Dismissal

[411]

(i) Collective dismissal is the termination of the employment of a large number of employees within a thirty-day period either by notice served by the employer on grounds specified in paragraph [408] (iii) (a) to [408] (iii) (c) or by agreement on the same grounds, provided that in the latter case at least five employees are served notice. A 'large number' of employees is considered to be at least:
  – 10 employees, if the employer employs between 20 and 100 employees;
  – 10% of the employees, if the employer employs between 101 and 300 employees; or
  – 30 employees, if the employer employs more than 300 employees.

(ii) At least thirty days before giving notice to individual employees, the employer is required to inform the competent trade union body or employee council of its intention. At the same time, the employer is required to enter into negotiations with these bodies on measures to avoid the collective dismissal or mitigate the negative consequences thereof for the employees, and in particular on the possibility of their employment in other suitable positions with the employer. Even though the objective of such negotiations is to reach an agreement between the employer and the trade union body or employee council, failure to reach any such agreement does not prevent any collective dismissal.

(iii) If there is no trade union body or employee council active at the employer, the employer is required to fulfil the above obligations in respect of each employee to whom the collective dismissal applies.

(iv) The employer is further required to inform a competent Employment Office in writing two times, first time about its intention to carry out a collective dismissal and second time to deliver to the office a written final report on its decision to issue a collective dismissal and on the outcome of negotiations with the trade union body or employee council. In the report, the employer must specify the total number of its employees and the number of employees and positions to which the collective dismissal applies. If the employer does not fulfil this obligation towards the Employment Office, the collective dismissal is ineffective. It will remain ineffective until expiry of at least thirty days after the delivery by the employer of its report to the Employment Office.

Participation of Trade Unions in Termination of Employment

[412]

(i) Trade unions that are active within the employer participate in the termination of employment if the employer wishes to dismiss an employee by notice or by immediate cancellation.

(ii) If the employer wishes to dismiss a trade union officer, then the employer must seek the prior consent of the trade union to such dismissal. Consent is also considered to have been given if the competent trade union body does not refuse in writing to give its consent within fifteen days of the day on which the employer asks for it. The dismissal of a trade union officer without the trade union's consent is invalid. However, the employer may claim in court that such dismissal is valid even without the trade union's consent if all other prerequisites for termination are satisfied and it would be unjust to require that the employer continue to employ such trade union officer.

(iii) If the employer wishes to dismiss an employee other than a trade union officer, it may do so without the trade union's consent. However, the employer must discuss each notice or immediate cancellation with the trade union before the notice or immediate cancellation is served. A breach of this obligation does not render the dismissal invalid, but may result in a fine of up to CZK300 000 (approx. EUR11 000) being imposed on the employer by the Work Inspectorate.

Severance Payment

[413] If employment is terminated by notice given by the employer for reasons cited under paragraph [408] (iii) (a) to [408] (iii) (c) or by agreement for the same reasons, the employee is entitled to a severance payment in the amount of:

(i) one month's average salary if the employment has lasted less than one year;
(ii) two months' average salary if the employment has lasted between one and two years;
(iii) three months' average salary if the employment has lasted two years or longer; and
(iv) three months' average salary, plus one of the sums under (i) to (iii) in special cases when a 'working hours account' (in Czech: '*konto pracovní doby*') is applied.

[414] For details regarding severance payment in the event of immediate cancellation on the part of the employee (i.e., an employee 'walks out'), please refer to paragraph [410].

[415] If employment is terminated by notice given by the employer for reason cited under paragraph [408] (iii) (d) or by agreement for the same reason, the employee is entitled to severance payment in the amount of twelve months' average salary.

[416] The employer may grant a higher severance payment to its employees under either collective bargaining agreements, the employer's internal regulations, or individual contract.

Employment Representatives

[417] Employees can form either trade unions or work councils as their representatives in employment relations. Alternatively, they may not be represented, in which case the employer must fulfil certain duties (e.g., the duty to inform) towards all employees directly.

Trade Unions

Basic Principles

[418] The basic principles under which trade unions operate in the Czech Republic are the following: (i) trade unions can be established irrespective of the will of the employer or the state authorities; (ii) they represent all the employees of a particular employer, irrespective of their will to be so represented; and (iii) it is forbidden to restrict in any way the establishment of trade unions or membership of a trade union, or for an employer to favour any trade union within a particular company or industry.

[419] In the Czech Republic, approximately 25% of all employees are currently trade union members.

Establishing a Trade Union

[420] A trade union may be established by at least three employees, of whom at least one must be aged 18 or over. A trade union becomes a legal entity with its registration with the relevant registration court. The court does not decide on the establishment of a trade union. It simply registers its existence, provided that all the required documents are submitted. Upon its registration with the registration court, the trade union is established and assumes all the authority granted to it by legal rules and regulations.

[421] Trade unions operate at company level, but can also form sizeable organisations (so-called confederations) which operate nation-wide.

Employee Councils

[422] As of 1 January 2001, the Labour Code has provided for the establishment of employee councils. An Employee council represents the employees of an employer. The employee council may coexist together with a trade union by an employer.

[423] The employer is obliged to organise elections to the employee council upon the petition of at least one-third of the employees. The employee council is duly elected only if more than one half of the employees participate in the elections. An employee council must have at least three, and at most fifteen, but always an odd number of members. The final number of employee council members is determined by the employer after negotiations with the employees' representatives for the purpose of the elections. The term of the office is three years. Employee councils always operate within one employer. They cannot establish *supra*-departmental structures.

[424] An employee council operates as a mediator between the employer and the employees. Its powers are less extensive than those of a trade union. The employee council represents the employees in the exercise of their right to obtain information and their right of negotiation. Employee councils are not legal entities (i.e., they do not have any legal capacity). Also, employee councils do not have a right to collective bargaining or to execute collective agreements, and may not, therefore, employ extreme measures, such as strikes, to resolve collective disputes.

Role of Employee Representatives

[425] Czech law confers on the trade unions and, to a lesser extent, to employee councils a wide range of rights and tools for the protection of employees' interests.

Collective Bargaining/Collective Agreements

[426] Trade unions are the exclusive representatives of employees in collective bargaining and in the conclusion of collective bargaining agreements, regardless of whether those employees are members of a trade union. The trade union bodies execute these agreements on behalf of all employees, at the company level (company collective bargaining agreements) or at the industry level (so-called higher-level collective bargaining agreements).

[427] Higher-level collective bargaining agreements are binding on all employees and employers in the industry/business in question.

[428] If several trade unions operate side by side at an employer, the employer shall negotiate the collective agreement with all such trade unions.

[429] The procedural regulations governing collective bargaining, including the resolution of collective disputes, if any (including strikes), are contained in the Collective Bargaining Act. This Act, together with the Labour Code, regulates who is to conclude collective bargaining agreements and what types of collective bargaining agreements exist (in-company and higher – i.e., concluded between employer organisations and higher trade union bodies). A procedure is provided for collective bargaining, in particular, for its commencement, such that collective bargaining is commenced upon the submission by either party to the other party of a written proposal for the conclusion of a collective bargaining agreement.

Right to Obtain Information

[430] Under Czech law, employers must provide certain information to employees or employee representative bodies (e.g., information on the likely development of the employment situation and any contemplated structural changes at the company).

[431] The 'right to obtain information' means the provision of the necessary data from which the state of communicated fact can be explicitly ascertained and if relevant, an opinion regarding this fact can be formed. The employer must provide this information sufficiently in advance and in a suitable manner in order that the employees can consider it and express their position before any measure is implemented.

[432] If a trade union is active within a company, the employer must provide even more information to the trade union. The employer is obliged to inform the relevant trade union of, for example, any expected changes in the level of wages/salaries, the average wage, the company's economic and financial situation, and the work conditions and structure of the workforce. The employer's power to decide at its own discretion remains unaffected by its obligation to provide information.

Right of Negotiation

[433] The employer is obliged to submit certain issues to the trade union and to the employee council for negotiation before deciding on such issues. In the event that no trade union and no employee's council exist within the company, the employer must negotiate directly with the employees. The right to decide on an issue remains exclusively with the employer but failure to negotiate with the trade union may be penalised by the relevant Work Inspectorate.

[434] The right of negotiation means negotiation between the employer and the employees and the exchange of views and explanations with the objective of reaching an agreement. The undertaking shall arrange for a consultation to take place sufficiently in advance and in an appropriate manner so that the employees can express their views on the basis of the information supplied and these views might be considered before the measure is implemented by the employer. The employees have the right to be provided with a reasoned response to their views. Before the implementation of the measure in question, the employees have the right to demand sufficient information and explanations. The employees also have the right to demand personal negotiations at the appropriate management level, depending on the nature of the matter. The employer, employees and the employee representatives are obliged to cooperate and proceed in line with their justified interests.

[435] Czech law provides an exhaustive list of those matters that the employer is obliged to negotiate with the trade union body. The employer is obliged to negotiate, for example, the employer's economic situation, employees' working conditions, changes in work organisation, employee assessment, remuneration, training, and all measures relating to a high number of employees. The law does not specify what constitutes a high number of employees. This must be decided on a case-by-case basis.

Right to Decide Jointly

[436] Another power enjoyed by the trade unions is the right to decide jointly with the employer on certain matters. Czech law provides an exhaustive list of these matters. This list may not be expanded by a collective bargaining agreement.

[437] Joint decision-making means that certain measures proposed by the employer may only be introduced with the prior consent of the relevant trade union body. If the employer fails to receive such prior consent, then its decisions are invalid.

[438] The most important issues in respect of which the employer must obtain the prior consent of the trade union is the termination (including the immediate termination) of the employment of an employee who is a trade union officer (during his/her term of office and one year thereafter), unless such employee agrees to the termination.

Right to Decide

[439] In certain cases, set forth by law, trade unions make decisions themselves. Such decisions are binding on third parties.

[440] Trade unions decide independently on, for example, matters related to their establishment, internal structure, activities, assets, membership fees, and the possible employment of employees for their own needs. A trade union acts as an employer towards its employees and provides them with remuneration.

[441] Trade unions may decide instead of the employer on certain matters expressly stipulated by law relating to health protection and operational safety, but only if the employer is in breach of the respective regulations.

Right of Supervision

[442] Trade union bodies are authorised to supervise the employer's observance of:

- the Labour Code;
- the Employment Act; and
- control of health and safety in the workplace.

[443] In conducting supervisory activities with respect to health and safety in the workplace, the relevant trade union bodies are authorised, in particular, to enter the employer's workplace, to require the provision of necessary information and supporting documentation, to inform the relevant Work Inspectorate and to propose that the Work Inspectorate review the measures taken by the Work Inspectorate, to take steps in relation to the employer in order to remedy possible defects, etc.

Particular Aspects Related to Acquisitions

Share Transaction

[444]

(i) If an acquisition is structured as a share transaction, the identity of the employer remains unchanged. A share deal will not affect the existing employment or any of the mutual rights and duties under existing employment contracts.

(ii) In a share transaction, in general, a trade union active within the employer has no co-decision or supervision rights in relation to the transaction, and the employer has no duty to inform the trade union (or any other employee representatives) about the transaction, unless it would affect employees.

Asset Transaction

[445]

(i) A different regime applies to an asset transaction in which the employer changes during the transaction. In such case, all employment contracts pertaining to the acquired business transfer to the purchaser by operation of law, and no modification to the employment contract is required. An asset deal as such does not trigger the transfer of employment. Rather, this happens only if the original employer's activities are transferred.

(ii) The Civil Code stipulates that if an enterprise or a part thereof is transferred to a new owner, all employment which existed at the time of the transfer and pertaining to the enterprise or the part transferred shall pass to the new owner by operation of law. The contract must be in writing and the parties must comply with other conditions prescribed by Czech law.

(iii) The provisions of the Civil Code on the sale of an enterprise or a part thereof are reflected in the Labour Code, which provides even stricter protection to employees than the 'Acquired Rights' Directive (i.e., an automatic transfer is triggered in more situations). If an enterprise or a part thereof or some of the employer's activities are transferred to another employer, all rights and obligations arising from the employment or affected employees are transferred to the new employer. The original employer's rights and obligations towards employees whose employment was terminated before the day of the transfer remain unchanged.

(iv) The employer is obligated to negotiate the transfer with either the trade union or employee council. If there are no such employee representative bodies, the employer must inform the employees affected by the transfer about the transfer directly. The negotiations must take place or information be provided at least thirty days before the transfer is realised. Although the negotiations must take place, they do not need to lead to consent.

(v) The employees can prevent themselves being transferred to a new employer. If they serve termination notice to the employer in relation to the planned transfer prior to it being realised, their employment terminates with the expiry of such notice period (however, no later than on the day preceding the transfer).

Employment of Foreigners in the Czech Republic

[446] All foreigners (except citizens of Member States of European Union, European Economic Area and Switzerland, including their family members) without permanent residence in the Czech Republic must obtain a relevant permit in order to be allowed to stay and work in the Czech Republic.

Employment by Local Entity

[447] If a foreigner is coming to the Czech Republic to become an employee of a Czech employer, such employment is possible only if the employer has notified the Czech Labour Office of such work vacancy and if the employee has obtained a so-called Employee Card, which serves both as a work and residency permit. An employee may apply for an Employee Card at the relevant Czech Embassy or (in some cases) in the Czech Republic at the Ministry of Internal Affairs. The intention of the authorities is that the whole process should take approx. four months; however, usually it takes longer.

Secondment of an Employee to the Czech Republic

[448] If a foreigner is seconded by a foreign employer to work temporarily at a Czech employer, such secondment is possible only if the employee has obtained (i) a work permit issued by the Czech Labour Office and (ii) an Employee Card (serving as a residency permit) issued by the Czech Ministry of Internal Affairs. The work permit must be applied for at the Czech Labour Office, in close cooperation with the local employer, and the Employee Card must be applied for at the relevant Czech Embassy or (in some cases) in the Czech Republic at the Ministry of Internal Affairs. The whole process should take approx. three to four months, however, usually it takes longer.

INTELLECTUAL PROPERTY RIGHTS

[449] Intellectual property rights recognised under Czech law can be broadly divided into two groups. Copyright (and related rights) covers artistic and creative works, while industrial property rights protect knowledge with an industrial application.

Copyright

[450] Copyright and its related rights are regulated primarily by Act No. 121/2000 Coll., the Copyright Act, as amended (the '*Copyright Act*'). The Copyright Act regulates the following types of rights:

(i) copyright of the author to Copyrighted Works (as defined below);
(ii) related rights to copyright; and
(iii) the right of the person compiling a database to such database.

Copyrighted Works

[451] Under the Copyright Act, copyright protection is extended to literary and other artistic and scientific works which are the unique result of the author's creative activity and are expressed in an objectively perceivable form (including electronic form), whether permanent or temporary and without regard to its extent, purpose or meaning ('Copyrighted Works'). The definition of Copyrighted Works further includes computer programmes, and databases.

[452] By contrast, in and of themselves, daily reports or other data, ideas, processes, principles, discoveries, scientific theories, mathematical formulas and statistical graphs are not considered Copyrighted Works. Furthermore, no protection is extended to public works (e.g., legislation, court decisions or public documents) and to folklore works whose authorship is unknown.

Creation of Copyright and Authorship

[453] Copyright is created by the operation of law at the moment when the Copyrighted Work in question is first expressed in any objectively perceivable form. No registration is possible.

[454] The author of a Copyrighted Work is always the natural person who created the Copyrighted Work. In the event of a collective Copyrighted Work (e.g., a database or a compilation), the author is considered to be the person who selected or organised the individual elements in a creative manner. The Copyright Act stipulates the presumption (which is open to challenge in the courts) that the author of the Copyrighted Work is the person whose name is listed on the Copyrighted Work.

Rights of the Author

[455] The author of any Copyrighted Work has moral and economic rights.

[456] The moral rights of the author include the right to (i) decide on the publishing of the Copyrighted Work; (ii) claim authorship; (iii) decide on any modifications that may interfere with the integrity of the Copyrighted Work; and (iv) maintain the integrity of the Copyrighted Work. We note that the moral rights of the author are inalienable, may not be waived and terminate upon the death of the author.

[457] The economic rights of the author extend to the usage (i.e., copying, publishing, renting, exhibiting or broadcasting) of the Copyrighted Work by the author and to the granting of a licence to use the Copyrighted Work to third persons. The Copyright Act specifies several exemptions where no licence is needed (such as a private copy exemption, library exemption, news exemption). We note that the economic rights of the author are inalienable, may not be waived and cannot be subject to the enforcement/execution of a decision. There are some cases when the rights of the author are limited by operation of law (e.g., an employer is exercising any and all economic rights of its employees).

Protection and Enforcement of Copyright

[458] The author may protect and enforce copyright via the courts in the event that there has been an infringement of his right or in the event of an impending infringement of his rights.

[459] The author may request in particular the following:

(i) determination of authorship;
(ii) a cease and desist order designed to prevent or stop the impending, ongoing or repeated infringement of the author's rights; in order to protect the

author from an ongoing infringement such an order may also be issued as a preliminary injunction;

(iii) provision of information on the type and scope of the infringement and on the source, price and resulting income from any unauthorised copies;

(iv) elimination of the consequences of the infringement (e.g., by a recall of unauthorised copies from the market and/or the destruction of any unauthorised copies);

(v) compensation for non-material loss by way of an apology or (where an apology is not sufficient) monetary compensation; the amount of the compensation is determined by the court, considering the severity of the infringement and the particular circumstances of the case;

(vi) compensation for damage – includes material damage (which is unlikely) and loss of income; compensation for loss of income can be provided by paying the typical price of the licence for which the infringing party should originally have paid; and

(vii) compensation for unjust enrichment – the amount is presumed to be double the typical price of a licence; a claim for unjust enrichment usually excludes a claim for damages.

[460] In the event that an exclusive licence is granted by the author, the licensee is the only person authorised to bring claims under (ii) –(iv), (v) and (vi) above.

[461] The Copyright Act also provides for the creation of collective rights organisations, which may assist authors with the protection and enforcement of their copyright. Membership of such organisations is generally voluntary; however, the collective rights organisations are exclusively responsible for the collection and distribution of certain types of royalties.

[462] Claims for protection of copyright are decided by the Regional Courts.

Due Diligence Verification

[463] Due to the fact that it is not possible to register copyright in the Czech Republic, its verification during the course of any due diligence must be made on an individual basis.

[464] Wherever the use of copyright is identified, the relevant company should be able to demonstrate its right to use such copyright, either by virtue of authorship or of a licence. We note in this context that licence agreements do not necessarily have to be made in writing (with the exception of exclusive licences). However, the existence of a verbal or implied licence agreement would have to be proven by a user, if challenged by the author.

[465] A particular issue encountered in real estate transactions is the right of the architect to the protection of his Copyrighted Work (i.e., the design of a building). Where an architect does not give his consent to structural changes to the design (e.g., in the form of reconstruction or the construction of annexes) beforehand, such structural changes may lead to a violation of the architect's moral right to the protection of his Copyrighted Work.

Special Rights of Use of Databases

[466] Databases may be considered collective Copyrighted Works, provided that the manner of selection or organisation of their content is the result of the author's own intellectual creative activity and that the database's elements are systematically or methodically organised and made accessible by electronic or other means.

[467] The author of a database does not have the full rights enjoyed by an author of a Copyrighted Work, as the author only has the right to mine the database and to grant access to the public. The author of a database may also grant licences to the above-mentioned rights. The rights of an author of a database are fully transferable. The manner of protection and enforcement of these rights is identical as for any other Copyrighted Works.

INDUSTRIAL PROPERTY RIGHTS

[468] Under Czech law, industrial property rights refer to (i) patents; (ii) utility models; (iii) industrial designs; (iv) trademarks; and (v) topographies of semiconductor products.

Registration of Industrial Property Rights

[469] All industrial property rights have in common the fact that they are only created by their registration with the Industrial Property Office (the *'IPO')*. For the purposes of such registration, potential rights holders must complete an electronic form (which is available on the IPO's website), attach to it the required additional documentation, and submit it to the IPO. Furthermore, a registration fee of approx. EUR20–500 (depending on the type of industrial property right being registered) must be paid by the applicant.

[470] During the course of the registration proceedings, the IPO verifies whether the basic legal conditions for the registrations are met. With respect to the individual types of industrial properties, these conditions could be summarised in the following manner:

(i) patents – inventions must be new, the result of scientific activity and commercially usable; in particular, scientific theories, mathematical methods, business processes, software, medical processes and therapeutic methods are not patentable;
(ii) utility models – technical solutions which are new, exceed the level of standard professional capacity and are industrially usable;
(iii) industrial designs – such designs (i.e., the visual look of a product) may be registered if the relevant design is new and has an individualised nature;

(iv) trademarks – any designation (words, pictures, numbers, colours, shapes, packaging) must enable the clear differentiation of a certain person's products or services from another person's products or services of the same kind; furthermore, a trade mark will not be registered if it is identical or similar to an existing trade mark in such a way that could be misleading to the public, provided an owner of the existing trademark files an objection to the registration of the new trademark with the IPO;

(v) topographies of semiconductor products – topographies may be registered if they are the result of the creative activity of their author and if they are not common in the semiconductor industry.

Protection and Enforcement of Industrial Property Rights

[471] The rights of the creators of industrial property rights generally extend to the use of their industrial property (i.e., to the production of products incorporating such industrial property and to the granting of a licence to do so to third parties). The rights holders may also fully transfer their industrial property rights to third parties.

[472] In the event of any infringement of their rights, holders of industrial property rights may demand:

(i) information on the origin and distribution networks of the infringing products;

(ii) a cease and desist order and the elimination of the consequences of the infringement (e.g., by means of the recall of unauthorised products from the market and/or the destruction of any unauthorised products or tools used for the creation of unauthorised products); and

(iii) compensation for damage, unjust enrichment and non-material loss (this may take the form of monetary compensation); the court may, upon the request of one of the parties, set the amount of such compensation at double the typical price of a licence (or at the typical price of a licence if the unauthorised user did not know and could not have known about the infringement).

[473] The above-mentioned claims may also be brought by a licensee, provided that the rights holder agrees or in the event that the rights holder does not enforce his rights for more than thirty days after an infringement has been notified to him by the licensee.

[474] Claims for infringement of industrial property rights must be filed with the Municipal Court in Prague.

Due Diligence Verification

[475] Due to the fact that all industrial property rights must be registered with the IPO, verification for due diligence purposes is relatively straightforward, as the registers of the IPO are generally searchable online.

[476] We note that transfers of industrial rights should also be registered with the IPO. While a failure to register a transfer with the IPO does not render such a transfer invalid, such a transfer would not be effective against third parties (e.g., any claims for infringement would have to be brought by the original rights holder). Similarly, licences only become effective against third parties by their registration with the IPO (this is relevant in particular with respect to exclusive licences).

ACCOUNTING TREATMENT

[477] The format and content of group accounts is determined by the Czech Accounting Standards and Decree on Double-Entry Accounting. In keeping accounting records a company should determine the content of the ledger accounts within the framework of the accounting chart provided by the Decree on Double-Entry Accounting. However, only the groupings (e.g., 'revenues from services' and 'business liabilities') contained in the accounting chart are mandatory.

[478] A company is obliged to maintain bookkeeping and prepare annual financial statements in accordance with International Accounting Standards if it has issued securities which are registered in a regulated securities market in one of the EU Member States.

[479] The accounting treatment of business combinations is determined by Czech Accounting Act and by the Act on Transformations.

Merger, Demerger, Squeeze-Out

[480] For accounting purposes, a transformation is effective as of its merger date.

[481] The involved companies are required to prepare ordinary or extraordinary financial statements as at the date preceding the merger date. Ordinary financial statements are prepared only if a day proceeding to the merger date is the same as the end of the regular accounting period. An accounting period shall either correspond to a calendar year or an economic year. If the Act on Transformations requires an expert valuation of the dissolved company's assets, this valuation is transposed to the financial statements of the successor company. The corresponding valuation difference increases or reduces the company's equity.

[482] The successor company(ies) are required to prepare an opening balance sheet as at the merger date. The successor company takes over (i) any evaluation difference (between, for example, the value of assets of the dissolving company and

the their newly evaluated value) in respect of acquired property; (ii) goodwill from previous transformations; (iii) adjustments to individual categories of assets; (iv) temporary assets and liabilities and (v) reserves recorded by the dissolved company only if the agreement between the companies (e.g., merger project or demerger project) provides for this.

[483] Special attention should be paid to mergers where one of the involved entities holds an ownership interest or shares in another involved entity (e.g., a merger of a parent company and its subsidiary). The value of the eliminated shares issued by a dissolved company(ies) reduces the equity in the opening balance sheet (of the successor company). If the company holding the eliminated shares is highly leveraged, the successor company may report negative equity as a result of the merger. This may have various indirect tax and legal consequences – for example in terms of the thin capitalisation rule.

Transformation of the Legal Form

[484] A transformation of the legal form has no impact on the valuation of the company's assets in its balance sheet.

[485] In the case of the transformation of a limited liability company, a joint-stock company or a cooperative into a general partnership or a limited partnership or vice versa, the company is required to close its books and prepare extraordinary financial statements which have to be audited.

Other Issues

[486] In the Czech Republic there is no special merger accounting or acquisition accounting. The book value of assets and liabilities, however, may differ from the tax values of assets and liabilities.

[487] The share premium or the difference between the value of assets of a dissolving company and their value as appraised during the merger of such company shall be booked into equity.

[488] The tax book values of assets and liabilities are not affected by any changes that result from the intentions of the acquirer or from events occurring after acquisition.

[489] Costs relating to the implementation of reorganisation are booked into the profit and loss account of the successor company.

[490] Under Czech Generally Accepted Accounting Principles(GAAP) there exist two possible ways for the recognition of the re-evaluation: by way of (i) goodwill and (ii) so-called re-evaluation difference.

[491] Goodwill is the difference between the valuation of a business and the sum of individually revalued asset items, reduced by transferred liabilities. Goodwill should be written off as expenses in the profit and loss account over the sixty months following the acquisition of the enterprise or the merger date of transformation. A company may decide on a depreciation period longer than sixty months, but such decision has to be explained in the notes on financial statements.

[492] Re-evaluation difference is the difference between the valuation of a business and the sum of the values of individual assets, reduced by liabilities that are assumed by the successor company. The re-evaluation difference should be written off as expenses in the profit and loss account over the 180 months following the acquisition of the enterprise or the merger date of transformation. Where acquired property in respect of which a re-evaluation difference is created does not involve assets with a useful life of more than 180 months, a company may decide on a depreciation period shorter than 180 months, but this fact has to be explained in the notes on financial statements.

[493] A company can decide either to (i) transfer the 'old' goodwill and then to amortise it or (ii) write it off. There is no possibility to regard goodwill as 'indefinite' and therefore not subject to amortisation.

[494] Intangible assets comprise in particular formation expenses, the intangible results of research and development, valuable rights, software, and goodwill with a useful life of more than one year, starting from the valuation amount determined by the company in question.

[495] The valuation of intangible assets shall be made at their acquisition costs. In the case of intangible assets generated by the company's own efforts, valuation shall be made at production costs.

[496] Generally, intangible assets are amortised over their useful life.

[497] In the case that an intangible asset (e.g., software) is re-evaluated due to a transformation, the successor company will amortise it from the re-evaluated price and over its 'new' useful life. If the intangible asset is not re-evaluated, the successor company will take over the residual value of asset and amortise it for its remaining useful life.

[498] Negative goodwill is recognised as a balance sheet item and is equally written off to revenues at the longest over 60 months (in the case of a negative re-evaluation difference, it is written off over 180 months) since the acquisition of the enterprise or the merger date of conversion.

[499] Acquisition costs are included as expenses in the profit and loss account in the accounting year in which they were incurred.

[500] The merger date of merger is defined as the day from which the actions of the dissolving company are considered, from the accounting and corporate income tax perspective, to be made on the account of the successor company. The merger date is determined by merging companies in the merger project.

[501] Deferred and contingent payments should be transferred for their fair (market) value.

[502] The vendor includes any profit arising on the sale in revenues (in its profit and loss account) for the period to which these revenues relate, taking into consideration their timing and nature. There are no differences between extraordinary and exceptional items.

Made in the USA
Monee, IL
13 September 2026

62974272R00083